LABCRAFT WIZARDS

MAGICAL PROJECTS AND EXPERIMENTS

JOHN AUSTIN

CHICAGO
REVIEW
PRESS

Copyright © 2017 by Austin Design Inc.
All rights reserved
Published by Chicago Review Press Incorporated
814 North Franklin Street
Chicago, Illinois 60610
ISBN 978-1-61373-621-0

Library of Congress Cataloging-in-Publication Data
Is available from the Library of Congress.

Labcraft Wizards is a trademark of Austin Design Inc.
All rights reserved

Cover and interior design: Jonathan Hahn
Illustrations: Austin Design Inc.

Printed in the United States of America
5 4 3 2 1

This book is lovingly dedicated to Henry, a magical blessing.

Love always, Dad

"Spell unto others as you would have them spell unto you."
—MOTTO OF THE SCHOOL OF LABCRAFT WIZARDS

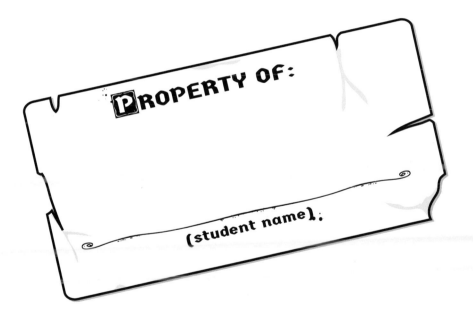

PROPERTY OF:

(student name):

Contents

Introduction

Labcraft Wizards is a mystical handbook for aspiring wizards that will show you how to transform everyday items into instruments of magic.

This collection of magical projects and experiments will be your primary guide as you begin your studies at the School of Labcraft Wizards. Whether your goal is to train for wizard duels, craft powerful artifacts, summon mythical creatures, or command the forces of nature, it will show you the way.

A novice wizard's studies can be overwhelming, but acquiring the supplies to practice magic shouldn't be. Each project in this book can be conjured by consulting a list of easy-to-locate materials and following the illustrated step-by-step instructions. The final chapter offers a small library of custom magical labels, perfect for sprucing up the finished projects. And for those interested in expanding their education beyond the magical realm, *Labcraft Wizards* also explores basic chemistry, encourages observation, speculation, and experimentation, and fuels the imagination.

Remember that because Labcraft Wizard projects are home-built, some experiments may need to be attempted several times, with students making adjustments and problem-solving.

Keep in mind that this book is for entertainment purposes only. It is written from the perspective that wizards and magic really exist, so some details may differ from actual facts. ***Please review the "General Safety Rules" on page xi for your personal protection.***

General Safety Rules

When exercising your magical abilities, be responsible and take every safety precaution. Using nonrecommended materials, assembling items improperly, mishandling tools, and not respecting heat and fire can all cause harm. Where indicated, adult supervision is required. Prior to starting a project, summon the appropriate safety equipment, especially safety glasses, and heatproof gloves or mitts when using fire.

Some of the projects outlined in this magical book require tools such as hobby knives, hot glue guns, and wire cutters that can cause injury if handled carelessly. ***Junior wizards should always be assisted by an adult when handling such tools.*** Tools need your full attention; make safety your number-one priority. If you have not used a particular tool before, ask someone to show you how to safely handle it. If you have trouble cutting, your knife may be dull or the selected material may be too hard; stop immediately and substitute one of the two.

Always be aware of your environment, including any non-magic bystanders. The advanced potion projects—Crystal Courage, Hot Ice, and Brew Slugs—require the heating of liquids to boiling. If mishandled, these projects can cause serious harm. Projects that require fire should never be attempted around flammable liquids, curtains, or curious house trolls. ***Some projects require ingredients that are harmful or could cause property damage. Read all ingredient labels when handling.***

I, _____, understand that safety is my
(WIZARD'S NAME)

number-one priority.

NOTE TO SUPERVISING ADULTS: Ensure that your young wizard is always responsible and properly supervised when constructing the projects in this book. It is important that you understand that the author, the publisher, and the bookseller cannot and will not guarantee the projects' safety. Those who attempt the projects described here do so at their own risk.

Instruments of Magic

Hot Glue Magic Wand

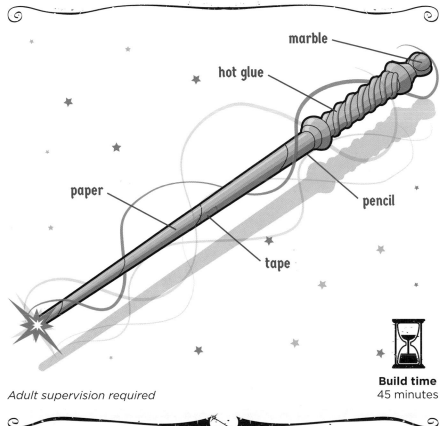

marble

hot glue

paper

pencil

tape

Build time
45 minutes

Adult supervision required

The Hot Glue Magic Wand is perfect for students who are just entering the world of magic. Constructed from everyday materials, this magic wand is both customizable and quick to assemble, making this a project perfect for mass production and outfitting a classroom full of wizards.

Supplies

1 sheet of copy paper (8½ by 11 inches)
Clear tape or masking tape
1 unsharpened wooden pencil
1 marble or similar small trinket
Craft paint (brown suggested)

Tools

Hot glue gun
Pliers (optional)
Paintbrush

Step 1

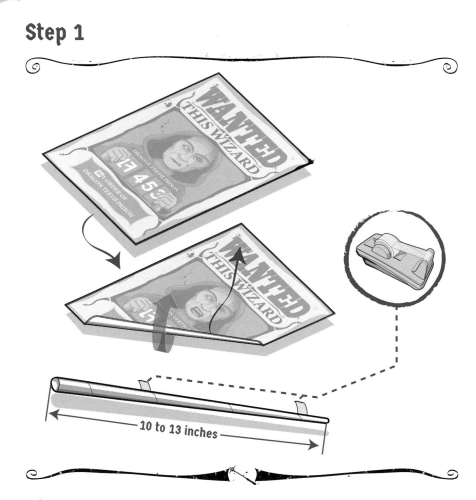

10 to 13 inches

On a flat surface, slowly roll an 8½-by-11-inch sheet of copy paper (or an old wizard wanted poster) into a tight paper cone. When finished, one end should come to a point, while the other end should have a ¼- to ½-inch opening in it.

Once it's tightly rolled, use clear tape or masking tape along the side of the cone to fasten it in place. The finished cone will be roughly 10 to 13 inches long.

Step 2

11 to 15 inches

Slide an unsharpened wooden pencil into the open end of the paper cone, with the eraser end facing out. Wedge the pencil into the tip of the cone until the combined assembly is 11 to 15 inches long. No two magic wands are identical, so the total length of the assembly may vary.

Secure the pencil by adding some hot glue to the open end of the paper cone, around the wedged pencil. Additional hot glue can be used to strengthen the wand tip as well.

Step 3

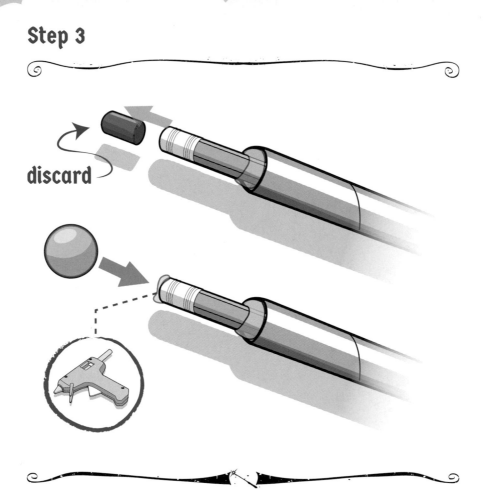

discard

With your fingers, dislodge the pencil's eraser from the metal band that holds it in place. Pliers may be necessary if the eraser refuses to budge. Avoid bending the metal band when removing the eraser.

Add hot glue to the inside of the empty metal band, and then attach a small marble, stone, or acorn, or a similar small trinket. Add more hot glue around the bottom of the attached item for increased strength.

When dry, the attached item will serve as the wellspring of your wand's mystical powers—and the ideal base for your wand's finger grip!

Step 4

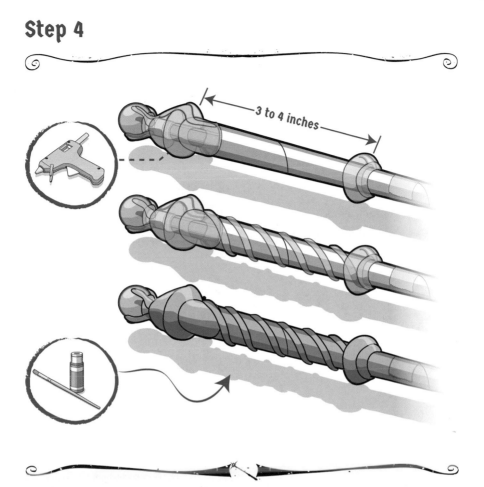

3 to 4 inches

With the glue gun, add front and back grip details approximately 3 to 4 inches apart as shown in the top illustration. As the glue dries, increase the thickness of the new grip details by adding several additional layers of hot glue. If desired, you can also add glue supports that grasp the sides of the marble, as indicated.

With more hot glue, create custom textures around the grip area of the wand shaft, as shown in the middle illustration. Straight lines, a swirl pattern, or an organic, wood-like texture are all fun possibilities.

When the hot glue has dried, use craft paint to add some color.

Step 5

Introduce yourself! Wield your wand by gripping the end with the same hand you write with. Rotate your wrist to move the wand in a clockwise *U*, then thrust it forward and confidently speak the incantation **"Fond companios!"**

Sculpted Magic Wand

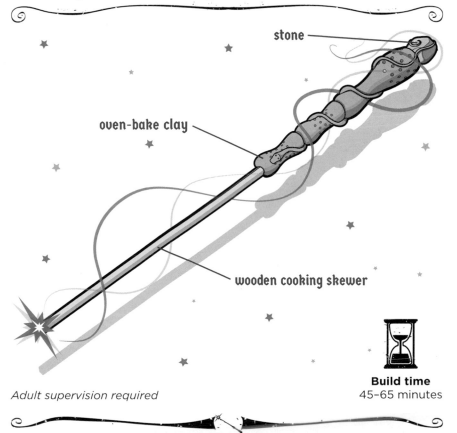

stone

oven-bake clay

wooden cooking skewer

Adult supervision required

Build time
45–65 minutes

No two wands are identical—each has a magical signature that is as unique as the wand's sculpted shaft. In this lesson, you will design and sculpt a wand that reflects your own personality, adding carvings, distinctive shapes, and magical items. With the right spark of inspiration, your creation may just go down in wandcraft lore.

Supplies

1 wooden cooking skewer
  (~12 inches long)
Oven-bake clay
1 small stone or other small
  trinket (optional)
Aluminum foil
Craft paint
Glitter (optional)
Black shoe polish (optional)

Tools

Safety glasses
Wire cutters or diagonal pliers
Cardboard (optional)
Wooden pencil (optional)
Cookie sheet
Ruler
Hot pad or oven mitt
Paintbrush

Step 1

The central shaft of this wand will be constructed from one wooden cooking skewer, roughly 12 inches long. While wearing safety glasses, remove the pointed end from the wooden skewer with a pair of wire cutters or diagonal pliers, as shown in the top illustration. Instead of a skewer, you can substitute a stick or wooden dowel that is similar in length.

Next, prepare a surface on which to roll out the clay, laying down cardboard if necessary. From a block of oven-bake clay, remove a piece that's roughly 2 inches wide, and roll it into a ball.

Once the clay is rolled, work it around the cut end of the wooden skewer, as shown in the bottom illustration, to create the handle of your wand. Sculpt the clay to create a unique handle design. *For baking purposes, it is important that the sculpted handle is no more than 1 inch thick at any point.*

Step 2

For more character, you can press a stone or other small trinket into the clay. Wandmakers add all types of items for their different magical properties. Be creative!

Continue customizing the handle by adding additional pieces of clay along the shaft of the wooden skewer. Use everyday objects as sculpting tools, such as the tip of a sharpened pencil to poke grip patterns that resemble serpent scales, as shown in the bottom illustration.

You can also use smaller bits of clay to add details, such as a small clay snake coiled around the handle. Just make sure no part of the design exceeds 1 inch in thickness.

Step 3

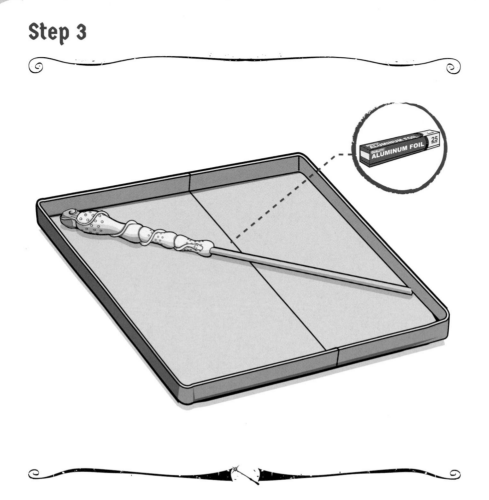

When sculpting is complete, preheat the oven to 250°F, or follow the manufacturer's recommended baking instructions. ***Baking should be done with adult supervision. Do not bake the clay in a microwave oven!***

Prepare a cookie sheet or other oven-safe cooking surface by covering it with aluminum foil. (The clay should never directly touch a baking surface also used for food.) Place the wand on top of the foil. Before baking, use a ruler to measure the maximum thickness of the clay.

Put the wand into the preheated oven and bake for 20 minutes for each ½ inch of thickness you measured. ***Do not increase the temperature to decrease the bake time.*** Higher temperatures could damage the clay and produce fumes.

Step 4

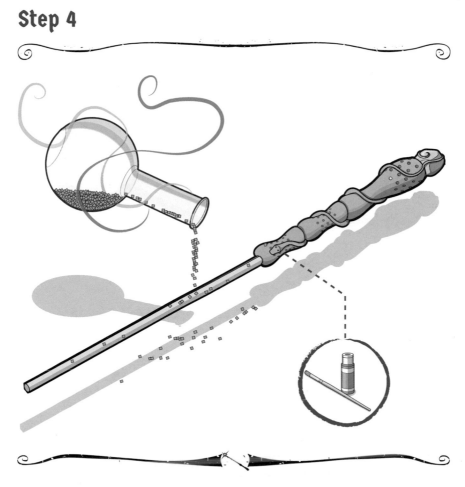

When baking is complete, use a hot pad or oven mitt to carefully remove the cookie sheet from the oven. Allow the wand to cool before touching. It is often said that when a wizard chooses the right wand it is warm to the touch—just make sure it's not *too* warm!

A wizard can add color to the wand by applying craft paint, which is preferable to spray paint because brushed-on paint can reach all the nooks and crannies carved into the clay. For a sparkling finish, you may want to sprinkle glitter onto the wet paint.

For added detail, after the paint has dried you can gently wipe a small amount of black shoe polish over the sculpted details. The polish will blacken the details, giving the wand the appearance of age.

Step 5

Congratulations, you have created a wand that suits your own magical character. Give the wand a try with the incantation **"Bastia mentalis,"** a telepathic protection spell.

Wand Box

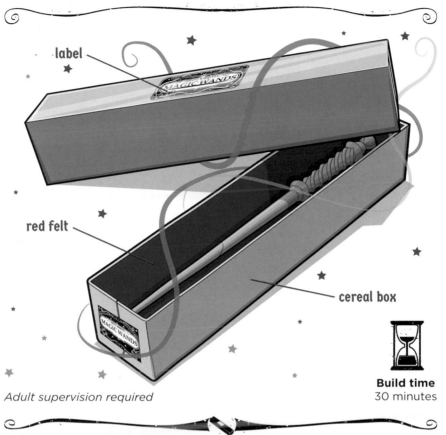

label

red felt

cereal box

Adult supervision required

Build time
30 minutes

Whether for display, storage, or stocking the shelves at a magic store, a Wand Box makes a great addition to any wandmaker's collection. Requiring little more than a repurposed cereal box and some magical cuts and bends, this project will enable you to stack hundreds of these cases to the ceiling in no time!

Supplies
1 large empty cereal box
Wand Box Labels (page 223)
1 piece of felt or sheet of construction paper (8½ by 12 inches)
White glue (optional)

Tools
Scissors
Ruler
Pen
Hobby knife (optional)
Safety glasses (optional)
Hot glue gun

Step 1

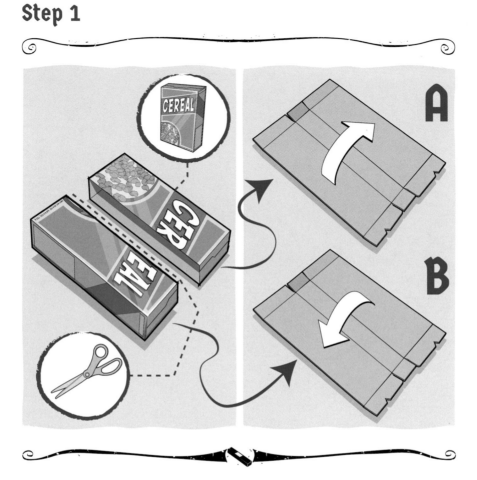

Start with a large empty cereal box, or a cardboard box that is similar in width and height. The original height of the cereal box will eventually be the width of the Wand Box, so to hold a 12-inch magic wand, choose a cereal box that's a little more than 12 inches tall.

With scissors, carefully cut the box vertically down the middle to create two identical halves, as shown (left).

Disassemble and flatten both halves of the box by carefully peeling apart the glued seams that hold the box together. Section A will become the bottom of the box and section B will become the lid.

Step 2

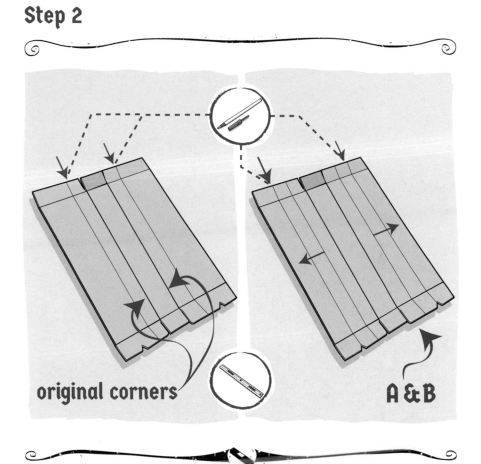

original corners

A & B

Look at the nonprinted side of flattened section A. You'll see two larger panels that used to be the front and back of the box, a narrower middle panel that used to be the side of the box, and between them the folded seams that formed the corners of the box. On each of the larger panels, use a ruler to measure and a pen to draw a guideline 1½ inches from the original corner seam. The two lines should be parallel and run the length of the box, as indicated on the left.

Next, measure and draw two additional lines 1½ inches from the first two guidelines, running the length of the box, as shown on the right.

Repeat this entire step for section B, so both cardboard sections have identical guidelines.

Step 3

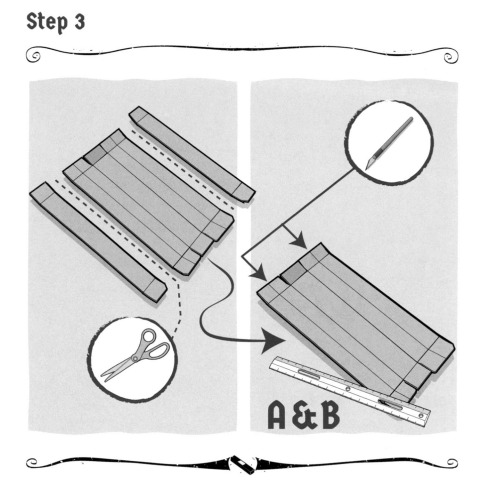

A & B

With scissors, cut along the two outside guidelines as shown at left. Discard the removed material. Repeat this step for both box halves, A and B.

With the ruler and a hobby knife or scissors (be sure to wear safety glasses if you're using a hobby knife), score the remaining two guidelines. That is, *do not* cut the lines all the way through—simply notch them with the blade, penetrating only half the width of the cardboard or less. Repeat this step for both box halves, A and B.

Step 4

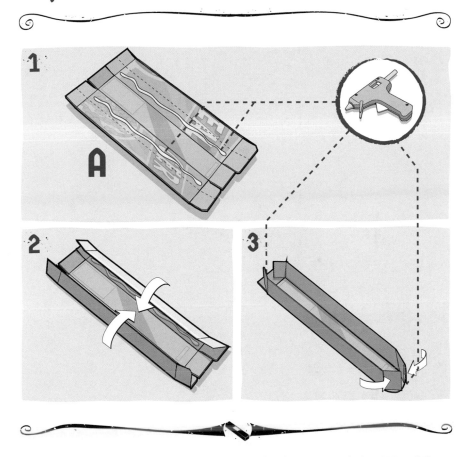

Now it's time to turn section A into the bottom of the Wand Box. Flip over the box so the printed side is facing up. Then add hot glue to the areas between the scored guidelines and the original corner folds on both side flaps, as indicated (illustration 1). Fold the two scored flaps inward (illustration 2); this creates two 1½-inch side panels of double thickness.

Fold the new side panels up to form the sides of the box (illustration 3). At each end, swing in the smaller side flaps, then fold up the larger bottom flap. Use hot glue to hold the flaps together. The bottom of the Wand Box is complete.

Step 5

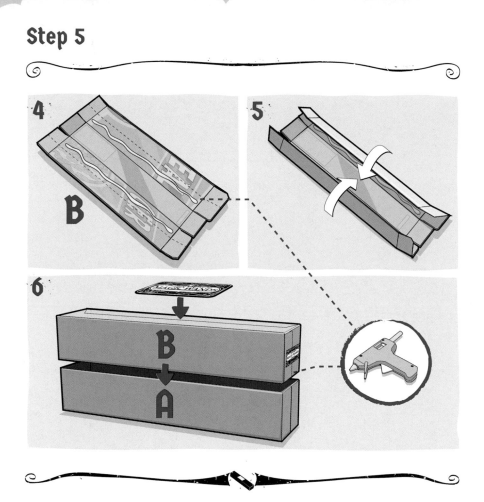

The cover of the Wand Box will be assembled from section B in a similar fashion. As with the box bottom, add hot glue to the areas between the scored guidelines and the original corner folds (illustration 4). Then fold the two scored flaps inward, to double the thickness of the outer walls (illustration 5).

Place the unfinished box top (B) over the completed box bottom (A) to ensure the proper fit (illustration 6). Once it's in place, hot glue the end flaps together to complete the box top. Be careful not to glue the top and bottom of the box together.

For an authentic touch, use hot glue to affix Wand Box Labels from chapter 7 (page 223).

Step 6

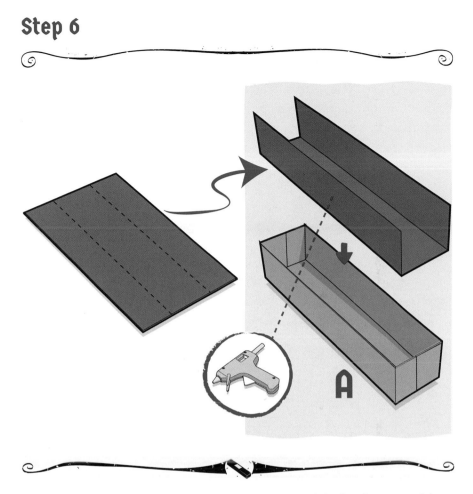

To protect the box's powerful contents and hide the cereal box graphics, you can use soft felt or colored construction paper to line the inside of the box bottom (A) as shown.

Use scissors to trim the lining to size, and prefold it for a snug fit. Use hot glue to secure felt and white glue for construction paper.

Step 7

Before you know it, you'll have 300 Wand Boxes completed! That amount might seem impossible to comprehend, but the best wandmakers have amazing memories. So while a wand shop might look cramped, dusty, and cluttered, the wandmaker is very aware of his or her magical inventory.

Enchanted Hourglass

plastic hanger

plastic bottle

masking tape

sugar

cardboard

Adult supervision required

Build time
30 minutes

Although meddling with the fabric of time is very dangerous and prohibited for all student spellcasters, some young wizards can't resist experimenting with spells that reverse, slow, and stop time. If you're experiencing bad déjà vu and fear you may be trapped in a temporal disturbance, reach for your Enchanted Hourglass, a device that renders the user impervious to all time-shifting spells.

Supplies
1 sheet of corrugated cardboard (18 by 10 inches)
Brown masking tape
2 clear plastic bottles (~16.9 fl. oz/500 mL each)
Paper towels
1 cup of sand, salt, or sugar
3 plastic clothes hangers

Tools
Marker or pen
Scissors
Hobby knife (optional)
Safety glasses
Single-hole punch
Hot glue gun
Wire cutters or diagonal pliers

Step 1

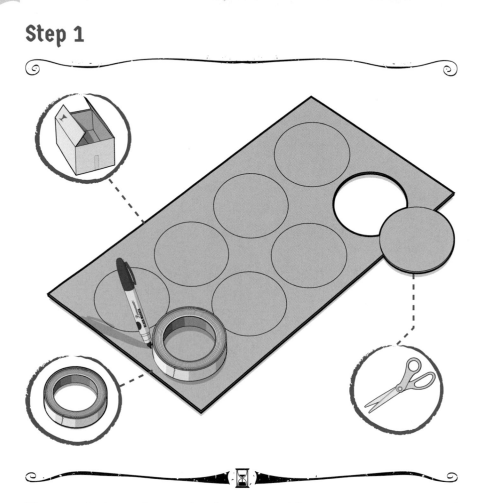

The magic hourglass's circular top and bottom are constructed out of stacked cardboard circles. To create them, first lay out a sheet of corrugated cardboard approximately 18 inches by 10 inches. Use a roll of masking tape as a template to ensure that all the circles are of equal size; it's critical that the diameter of the masking tape roll is *greater than the diameter of the two plastic bottles* you'll use in step 2. Lay the tape roll onto the cardboard and trace around it with a marker or pen *eight times*, as shown, to create eight identical circles.

Carefully cut out each cardboard circle with scissors. Stack the circles to confirm that they align with one another. Trim off any noticeable uneven edges.

Step 2

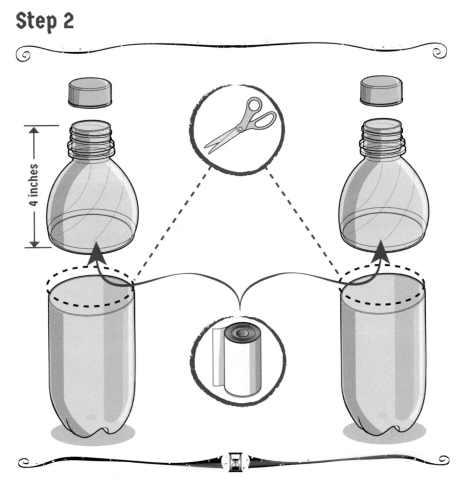

The Enchanted Hourglass will use two identical clear plastic bottles for its top and bottom sand bulbs.

With a hobby knife or scissors, safety glasses, and an adult's help, carefully remove the tops of both bottles by cutting each one 4 inches below the top threaded opening. Trim off any ragged edges on the bottle tops so that the cut edges are flat. The bottoms can be recycled or saved for the Magic Bean (page 187).

If the inside of either removed bottle top is damp, use a paper towel to dry it.

Step 3

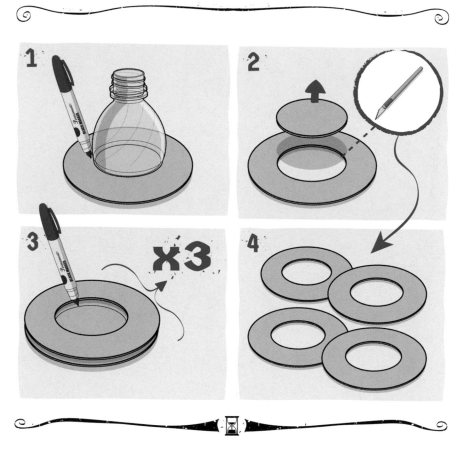

Center one of the removed bottle tops on one of the cut card-board circles as shown, then use a pen to trace around the edge, drawing a center ring on the cardboard (illustration 1). With the hobby knife or scissors, remove the drawn circle (illustration 2).

This cardboard ring will now be the template for three of your other cardboard circles. Place the ring on top of each circle and trace three more inner circles (illustration 3). Cut out the center of these three circles. When finished, you will have four rings (illustration 4), as well as four intact cardboard circles.

Save the cardboard scrap for step 5.

Step 4

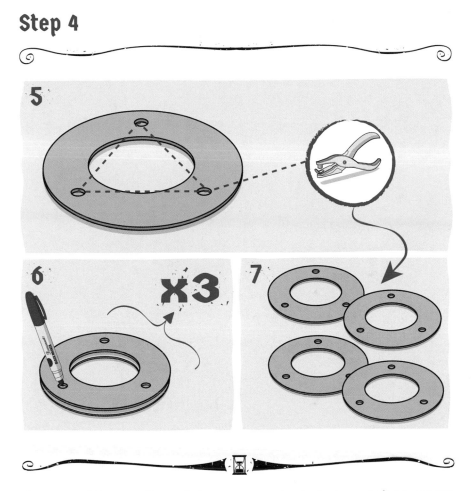

On one of the cardboard rings, use a single-hole punch to create three equally spaced holes around the outside of the ring (illustration 5).

Place the cardboard ring with three holes on top of each remaining cardboard ring, and use a marker or pen to indicate the placement of the holes (illustration 6). Punch these same holes out of the three remaining cardboard rings. When you're finished, you should have four matching rings (illustration 7).

Step 5

discard

Use a marker to trace the threaded bottle opening onto a scrap piece of cardboard, like one of the circular pieces removed during step 3, as shown on the left.

   Use scissors to cut out the small traced ring. Then use a single-hole punch to punch one hole directly in the center of this ring, as indicated on the right. Discard the rest of the cardboard scrap.

Step 6

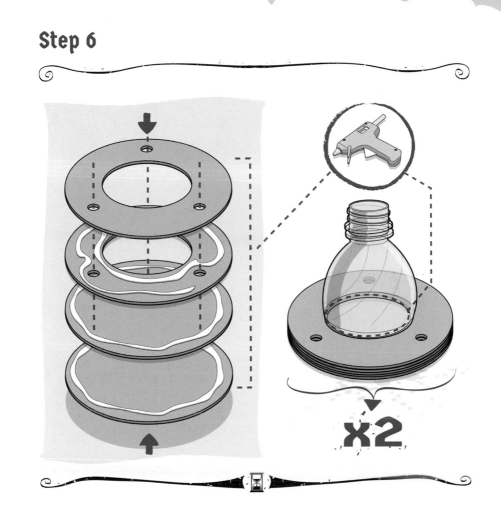

Time to assemble the Enchanted Hourglass! Each circular end will be built from four cardboard circles: two of the intact cardboard circles and two of the cardboard rings. With hot glue, sandwich two full circles together as shown, then glue the two rings on top of them, with the hole-punch holes aligning.

When the stack is dry, add more hot glue to the inside edge of the cardboard ring assembly, and then quickly wedge one of the cut plastic bottles into it.

Repeat this step with the remaining cardboard circles and second bottle top to create the other end of the hourglass.

Step 7

Pour dry sand, salt, or sugar into one hourglass half. *Do not fill it completely up*; it should only be about three-fourths of the way full.

Once the sand, salt, or sugar is in the bottle, hot glue the small cardboard ring onto the bottle opening as shown.

Step 8

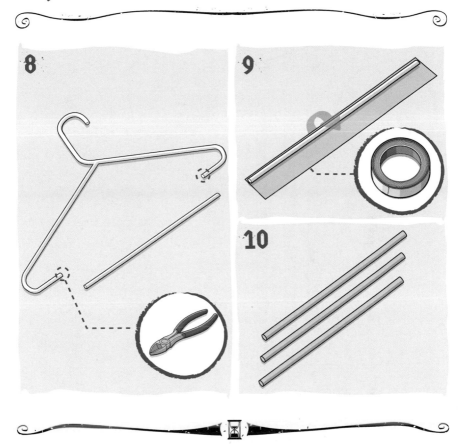

To protect the flowing sand during spell attacks, add three leg supports around the hourglass bulbs. The supports will be constructed from three plastic clothes hangers.

With a pair of wire cutters or diagonal pliers and an adult's help, remove the lower (long) bar from each clothes hanger by cutting it at both ends (illustration 8).

To match the color of the cardboard bases, wrap each plastic rod in brown masking tape by rolling the rod along the width of the tape as shown (illustration 9). Repeat this for all three hanger rods (illustration 10).

Step 9

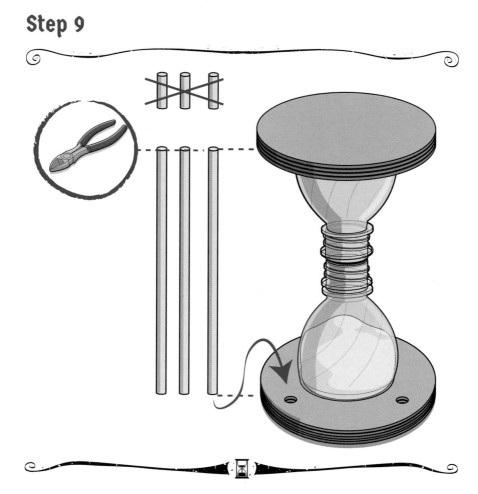

The hanger rod supports should be approximately 8¼ inches long, but hold them up to the stacked hourglass halves to determine the precise length they need to be to snugly fit into the hourglass. Be sure to add ¼ inch to your measurements so the supports will be long enough to extend into the holes punched into the cardboard rings. Use wire cutters or diagonal pliers to cut all three rods to the proper length.

Step 10

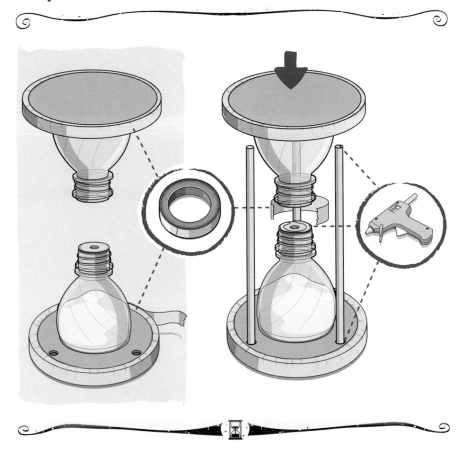

With brown masking tape, wrap the sides of both cardboard circles as shown to hide their corrugated edges.

Now it's time for the final assembly! On the hourglass base filled with sand, place hot glue in each of the holes punched into the cardboard, then insert the ends of all three clothes hanger rods, making sure they stand up straight.

Next, add a small amount of hot glue to the little cardboard cap on the filled hourglass half, but *make sure the glue doesn't block the opening*. Then quickly add glue to the three holes punched into the top hourglass half. Align the top holes with the rods and gently press them together, making sure the openings in the bottles align and are glued together as well. Wrap a few more pieces of masking tape around the bottle openings to hide the threaded edges.

Wait till all the glue is dry, then rotate the hourglass for testing.

Step 11

Novice wizards are often dared into friendly physical challenges such as Wobbly-Stooly, Double-Book Hat, and Uno Footy! Unscrupulous opponents may try to manipulate time to tip the scales in their favor. Keep the games honest by using an Enchanted Hourglass to repel all known time spells. Trust us, if you find yourself in a Woobly-Stooly-Uno-Footy double challenge, you'll be happy you listened.

Owl Craft

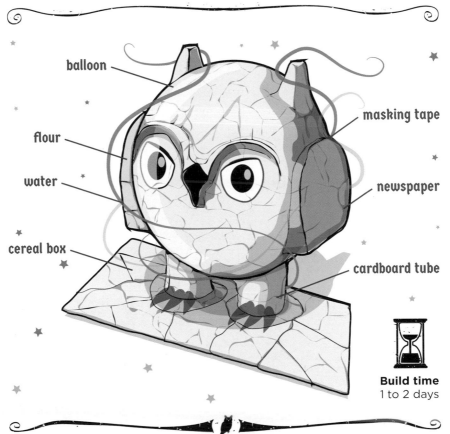

balloon

masking tape

flour

water

newspaper

cereal box

cardboard tube

Build time
1 to 2 days

Many spellcasters are assisted in their magical endeavors by an animal companion, sometimes known as a familiar. Young wizards often choose an owl for their companion animal. Fortunately, summoning your own owl is not difficult—but it is messy and fun!

Supplies

1 cardboard tube (12 inches long) or several toilet paper tubes

1 empty cereal box

Masking tape

1 large balloon

Newspaper

2 cups of water

2 cups of flour

Craft paint (optional)

Tools

Scissors

Large mixing bowl (8-inch diameter or more)

Wire whisk or fork (optional)

Marker

Step 1

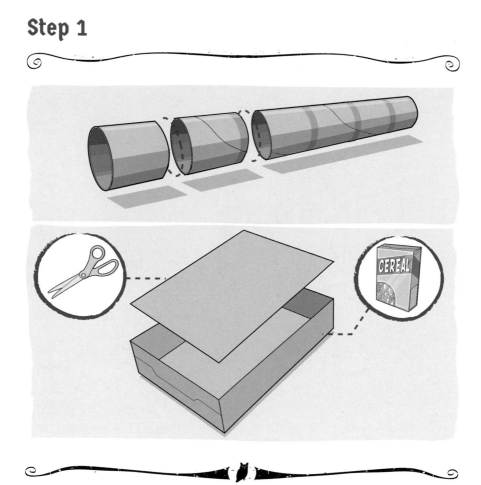

The owl's two legs will be constructed from a recycled cardboard tube—for instance, a paper towel or toilet paper tube. With scissors, cut two 2-inch sections off a larger cardboard tube, or cut one toilet paper tube in half.

Next, use the scissors to remove one large side from an empty cereal box or a cardboard box that is similar in size, as shown.

Step 2

Place both shortened cardboard tubes in the center of the removed cardboard square, approximately 1 inch from one another (illustration 1). Carefully secure both tubes to the cardboard with masking tape, as indicated (illustration 2).

To represent your owl's round body, inflate a large balloon to a diameter of about 8 inches and tie it off. Place the inflated balloon directly over the two attached cardboard tubes and fasten it in place with additional masking tape (illustration 3). During the paper-mâché process to come, the balloon will become very heavy, so secure it firmly.

Step 3

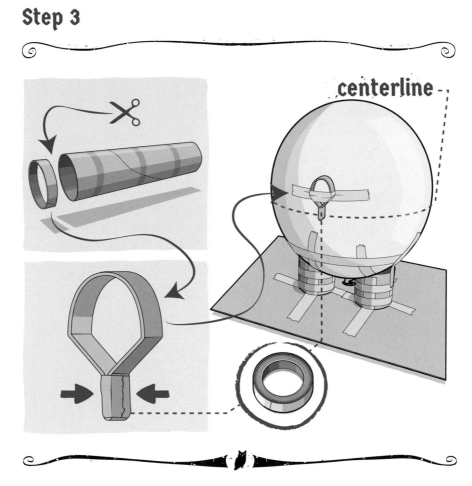

centerline

To create the framework for the owl's beak, cut a ½-inch cardboard ring from the remaining cardboard tube using scissors. Once it's removed, fold the cardboard ring into a tear shape as illustrated at bottom left. Hold this shape together by wrapping tape around the small point at the bottom.

Position the cardboard beak frame on the front face of the balloon, with the bottom point slightly above the balloon's centerline. Tape it in place.

Step 4

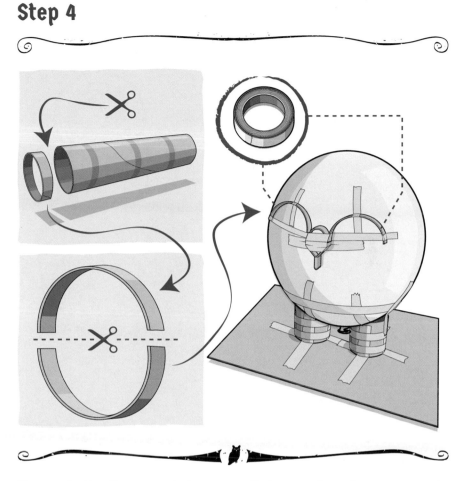

To create the framework for an owl's large, all-seeing eyes, again use the scissors to remove a ½-inch cardboard ring from the remaining cardboard tube.

Cut the ½-inch ring in half. Position the half-rings on the left and right sides of the attached beak frame as shown, with both cardboard halves arching upward to represent the owl's eyebrows. The tape should lie relatively flat against the surface of the balloon, but do not be overly concerned with its appearance, as it will eventually be covered with paper-mâché.

Step 5

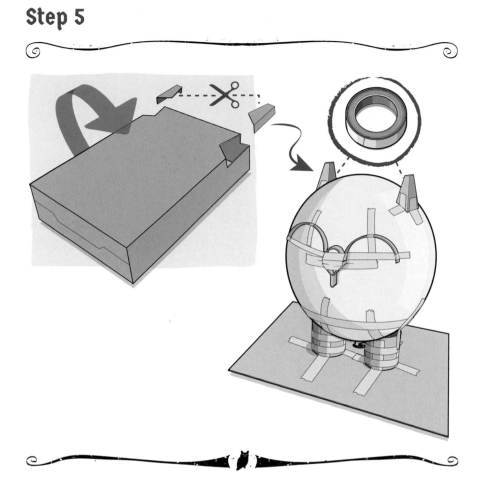

To give the owl ears, flip over the empty cereal box and cut out two box corners as shown. Each corner should be around 1 to 2 inches long.

Position both ears on top of the balloon, centered, directly behind the outer edge of the eyebrows. Use masking tape to keep them in place.

Step 6

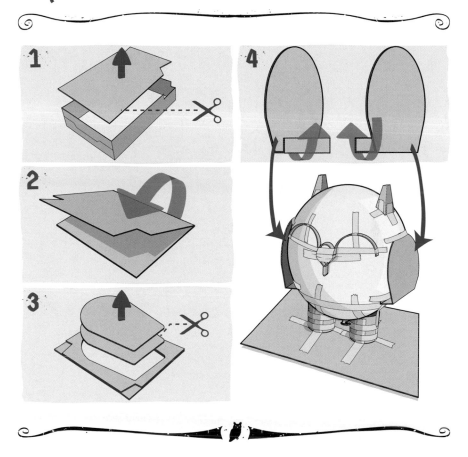

With scissors, cut the remaining large panel off the back of the cereal box (illustration 1). Fold the removed panel in half to create two equal sections (illustration 2). With the cardboard panel folded, use scissors to cut out two identical wing shapes. The wings should have a rounded top and flattened bottom and be roughly 5½ inches tall and 3½ inches wide (illustration 3).

Fold up each wing's flattened end two times, with the second fold roughly ½ inch from the first, as shown (illustration 4). Attach one wing to each side of the owl's body. Use masking tape to secure both wings into place, with the bottom tabs positioned to raise the lower edge of each wing off the balloon, as illustrated.

Step 7

2 cups   2 cups

Prior to mixing up the paper-mâché potion, cover your work surface with newspaper, cardboard, or a washable tablecloth. You will make a mess, so **get an adult's permission before proceeding**.

In a large mixing bowl, add 2 cups of water and 2 cups of flour. Mix the ingredients together with a wire whisk, a fork, or your hands until it resembles a creamy paste and is free of lumps. Additional water or flour may need to be added at this point or during the steps to come—add flour to thicken the mixture and water to thin it.

Step 8

The most common paper-mâché covering is newspaper, but tissue paper, paper towels, printer paper, and some magazine paper can be substituted. Tear the paper into strips of all shapes and sizes—the torn pieces do not need to be uniform. Create a large pile prior to dipping.

Dip a single strip of torn paper into the paste, coating the paper completely. Remove excess paste by running the wet strip between your thumb and forefinger. Then lay the strip flat against the owl's body. Repeat this step, overlapping the previous strip and covering more of the owl, until you have completely covered its body, its legs, and the cardboard base. The owl will need at least two layers of coverage.

When the owl is fully covered in paper-mâché, let it dry completely. It will take one or two days, depending on the number of additional layers applied.

Step 9

Use a marker or craft paint to give the owl eyes and a beak. If desired, you can add feather color with additional craft paint, picking a color scheme that allows your owl to reflect your own magical interests. An ice wizard might create a snow owl, white and mottled, while a nature wizard might prefer a wood owl, with feathers that look like tree bark.

Smoke Ring Launcher

pen

pushpin

vitamin bottle

balloon

Adult supervision required

Build time
45 minutes

A Smoke Ring Launcher is a clever device that sends small, swirling vortexes of smoke across the room. Magically manipulating the forces of fire and air is a skill usually reserved for elder wizards, so this project is sure to amaze your friends.

Supplies
1 empty plastic vitamin bottle
   (3½ inches tall)
1 balloon
1 pushpin
1 plastic ballpoint pen with
   cap
Spray paint or craft paint
   (optional)
1 incense stick

Tools
Hobby knife
Scissors
Safety glasses
Hot glue gun
Pliers (optional)

Step 1

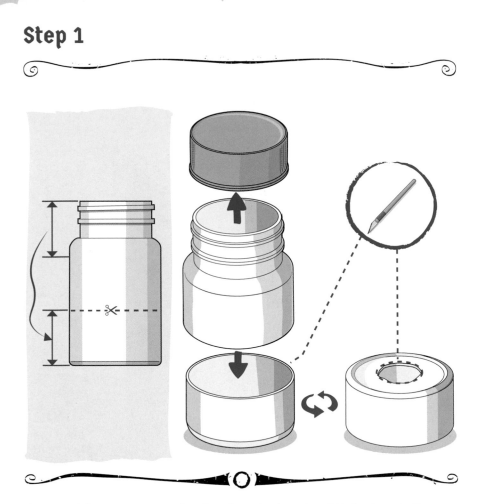

Start with an empty plastic vitamin bottle, 3½ inches tall, or a plastic container similar in size and shape (roughly 3 to 5 inches tall). If a suitable container is not available or you are looking for a quicker smoke ring launcher to build, see the bonus Smoke Ring Bottle project on page 51.

   With a hobby knife or scissors, safety glasses, and an adult's help, carefully cut apart the container 1 inch from the bottom (center illustration), a distance equal to the height of the threaded cap neck plus a little more (left illustration). Keep *both* plastic container halves to use in the construction.

   Flip over the lower section so that the bottom is facing up, and use a hobby knife to carefully cut out a small hole, ¾ inch in diameter, from the center (right illustration). The more circular and centered you're able to make the hole, the better your smoke ring quality will be.

Step 2

Use scissors to cut a balloon in half as shown. Discard the mouth end.

Slide the top of the balloon over the upper section of the vitamin container, starting at the cut end and stretching the balloon around the neck of the bottle.

Step 3

Apply hot glue around the bottle's threaded opening as shown (far left), then attach the upside-down bottom half of the container as a cap.

Next, add a handle mount to the side of the launcher. With scissors, remove the circular end from a plastic pushpin. Trim off as much of the plastic ring as possible (top right).

Mount the modified pushpin to the lower section of the launcher by pushing it through the balloon and the plastic housing (bottom right). You may need to add a bit of hot glue to hold the pushpin in place.

Step 4

Disassemble a plastic ballpoint pen into its various parts, removing the cap, the ink cartridge (and its plastic mount, if separate), and the rear pen-housing cap. Depending on how the pen has been manufactured, you may need small pliers or a disassemble spell to assist you in dislodging the rear pen-housing cap. With scissors, trim off a small wedge of plastic from one end of the pen tube. Then, at a 40-degree angle (see the angle illustration), test-fit the wedge end over the attached pushpin as shown.

Add hot glue to the inside of the wedge end of the pen housing, then slide that end over the pushpin. Once it's attached, add additional glue around the connection to hold in place.

When the glue is dry, it's time to add the end of the handle, made from the pen's cap. Bend the pen clip toward the cap opening at a 40-degree angle, as shown on the top right. Again, use the angle illustration to determine the bend. Use hot glue to secure the modified pen clip to the pen housing, and allow it to dry.

Step 5

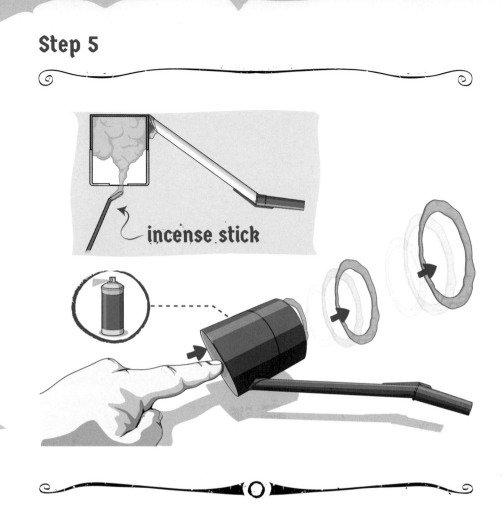

incense stick

The Smoke Ring Launcher is complete, but for a finishing touch, you can paint the launcher with spray paint or craft paint. Brown tones look especially nice. *Avoid painting the bottom surface, where the balloon is stretched across the opening.*

Now it's time for smoke vortexes! Light an incense stick to create smoke, then invert the launcher's opening over the rising smoke so it fills the launcher. Once it's filled with smoke, angle the opening away from you. With the tip of your finger, gently push the balloon bottom inward to create floating smoke rings.

This magical phenomenon can be explained by the way air molecules bottleneck as they're pushed out of a small hole. The air in the center of the hole is pushed forward, but the air along the edges backs up and begins circulating into a doughnut-shaped mass, creating what's called a *toroidal vortex*. The smoke suspended in the air makes this swirling visible as a ring.

Bonus

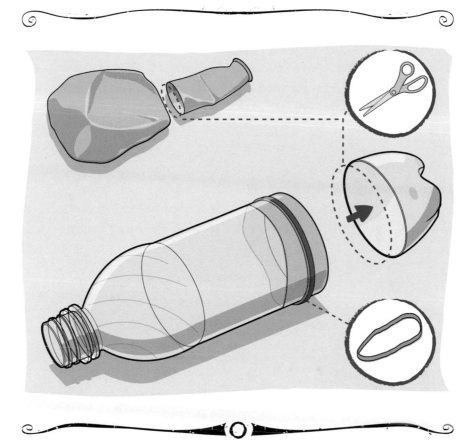

This Smoke Ring Bottle is a quick alternative design—great for when you're challenged to an unexpected Smoke Ring Duel!

Start with an empty plastic bottle (16.9 fl. oz./500 mL). With scissors, carefully remove the bottom of the bottle and discard it.

Next, use the scissors to cut a balloon in half, as shown above. Discard the mouth end. Stretch the remaining section of the balloon over the bottom of the bottle. Once the balloon is tightly stretched across the opening, use a rubber band or tape to hold it in place.

To use, see the instructions in step 5 for launching smoke rings.

Step 6

Unauthorized schoolyard duels are strictly forbidden, although the faculty have been known to ignore reports of students partaking in Smoke Ring Duels. If a student is challenged, best be prepared! Prior to the duel, the opposing wizards find a breeze-free location and agree on a number of playing cards to use as targets. The wizards are separated by a tabletop, roughly 4 feet from each other, and build one or more houses of cards in the center of the table. The incense stick or other smoke source is placed off to the side, an equal distance from each player. Wizards start blasting vortexes at the same time; the wizard who knocks over the most targets wins!

Mythical Creatures

Dragon Eggs

vinegar

food coloring

raw egg

Adult supervision required

Build time
24 hours

Traded in dark alleys, used to pay off debts, or hoarded by those who seek power, Dragon Eggs are worth their weight in gold. A fully grown dragon can transform any peasant into a conqueror, but caring for a Dragon Egg until it hatches can be just as difficult as acquiring one. These pages contain a simple protection potion that will give your Dragon Egg a magical bounce, and increase its size as well. Non-magic folk might call the result a Naked Egg or a Bouncing Egg.

Supplies

1 raw egg

1 cup of vinegar

Dragon Egg Label (optional, page 224)

Clear tape (optional)

Food coloring (a few drops)

Paper towels

Tools

Short drinking glass

Large spoon (optional)

Step 1

Scrounge around the school's glassware collection and try to locate a short, clear drinking glass suitable in size to fit one raw egg. Carefully set the egg inside the glass—if dropped, the eggshell could crack.

Next, locate some vinegar—if you can't find it next to the eye of newt and mandrake root, try the kitchen cupboards. Pour the vinegar into the glass until the egg is submerged. Don't be alarmed if it tries to float or if small bubbles suddenly appear on the surface of the shell; this is just carbon dioxide being released from the egg.

If you wish to warn curious classmates against disturbing this powerful ritual, you can tape a Dragon Egg Label (page 224) to the glass containing the Dragon Egg.

Step 2

24 hours

-wash & dry

Next, add a few drops of food coloring to the vinegar. Do you want a fearsome red dragon? A mysterious blue dragon? A majestic gold dragon (use yellow food coloring)? The choice is yours!

Hocus-pocus, it's time for osmosis! Let the egg sit in the potion for at least 24 hours. During this time, a chemical reaction will occur between the calcium carbonate in the egg's outer shell and the acetic acid in the vinegar, slowly dissolving the shell but leaving the inner membrane intact. That membrane is semipermeable, meaning that it will hold in the contents of the egg but allow certain substances to pass through via a process called *osmosis*. In this case, the semipermeable membrane will allow the colored mixture in the glass to be absorbed into the egg.

After 24 hours, carefully remove the egg with a large spoon, or slowly pour out the used vinegar. Use a paper towel to gently dry the egg off and remove any shell residue. You'll see that the absorbed liquid has caused the egg to grow!

Step 3

Wizard Warning: ***Do not eat dragon eggs!*** You should also handle them with care, as your protective brew will not prevent them from making a mess if the membrane is punctured.

Though the Dragon Egg is now finished, a curious wizard may want to attempt some additional experiments. For example, you can try to increase the Dragon Egg's size even more by soaking it in vinegar for another 24 to 48 hours. Another experiment: *shrink the Dragon Egg by soaking it in a cup of corn syrup for 24 hours.*

You can also test the results of your experiment against other wizards'. How far can your charmed Dragon Egg fall and bounce without exploding? Start the test at a height of 1 inch and increase the distance after each successful drop. *Conduct this duel outside or lay down a protective table covering to catch the mess when your eggs explode!*

Pixie Prints

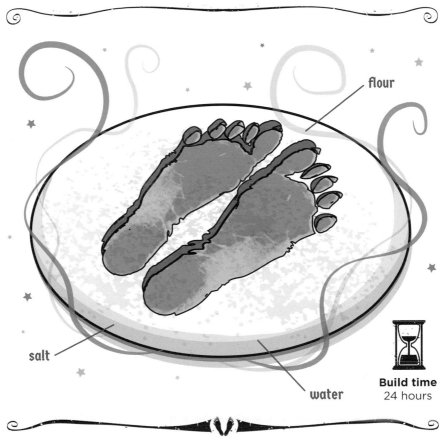

flour

salt

water

Build time
24 hours

Similar to fairies but larger and more mischievous, pixies can be difficult to capture for study. Fortunately, each pixie has a unique foot structure, and an astute wizard can learn all sorts of information just by examining the footprints they leave behind. It takes time for novice wizards to master the art of pixie footprint reading. So that you can practice at your leisure, your pixie's feet will be pressed into homemade plaster.

Supplies
1 cup of table salt
1 cup of plain flour
½ cup of warm water
Craft paint (optional)

Tools
Round mixing bowl
Spatula (optional)
Plate

Step 1

1 cup   1 cup

To start, find a suitable mixing bowl in the school's kitchen pantry. Add 1 cup of table salt and 1 cup of plain flour to the bowl. Swirl the two dry ingredients together using your hands. (Never use a wand to mix ingredients or you risk summoning the little-known Flour Ness Monster—a remarkably messy beast!)

Step 2

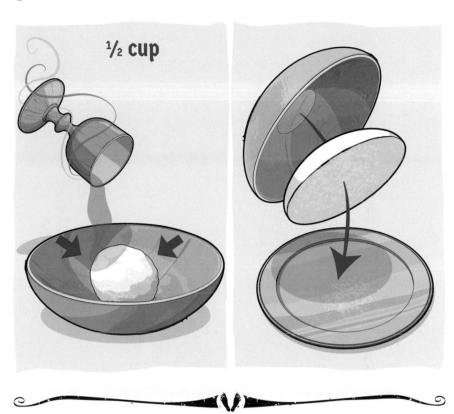

½ **cup**

Add ½ cup of warm water to the bowl. Mix all three ingredients together with your hands until the dough is smooth and pasty. If the dough seems dry and falls apart, add a small amount of additional water. If the dough is sticky, add a little more flour.

Create a dough ball as shown. Then press the ball into the bowl's rounded bottom and knead the edges until the surface of the dough resembles a neat circle.

Coax the edges slightly with your finger or a spatula and flip the dough onto a plate. The surface of the bowl has given the dough a smooth, rounded surface, perfect for making pixie prints in.

Step 3

Pixie feet are very small. To practice making prints, use your finger and/or the side of your palm to create tiny impressions in the rounded surface of the dough as illustrated. Set prints aside for 24 hours to let them harden. Once the prints are dry, you can use craft paint to help the footprints stand out.

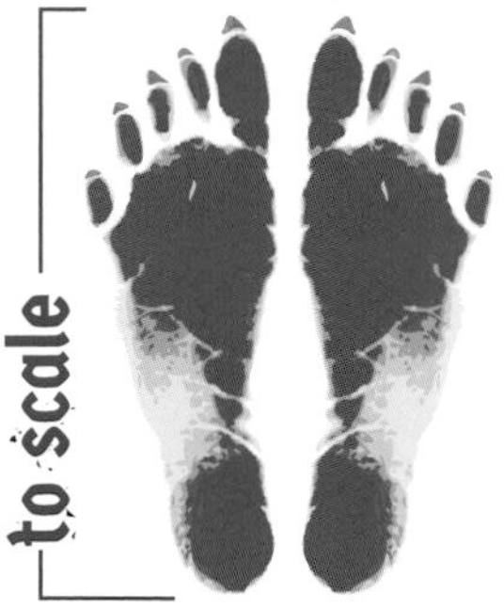

to scale

Ogre Snot

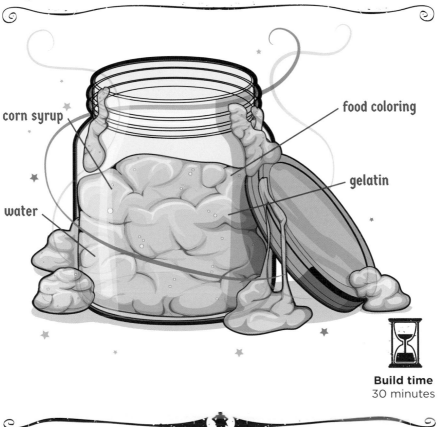

corn syrup

food coloring

gelatin

water

Build time
30 minutes

Ogre mucus possesses magical mending powers, and when applied to the skin it can heal magically induced ailments. Huge ogre noses produce huge amounts of Ogre Snot, but collecting a full jar of it can be a real pain in the nose! If you'd rather not run the risk of becoming an ill-tempered ogre's next meal, the following lesson plan reveals an easier way of acquiring this grotesque mucus-aid.

Supplies
½ cup of warm water
3 unflavored gelatin packets
    (0.25 oz. each)
½ cup of corn syrup
Food coloring (a few drops)

Ogre Snot Label (page 225)
Clear tape

Tools
Mixing bowl
Fork

Step 1

½ cup

3 packets

Gelatin
UNFLAVORED

Add ½ cup of warm water to a mixing bowl. Sprinkle three packs of unflavored gelatin (0.25 oz. each) into the bowl, spreading out the gelatin. Mix the gelatin and water with a fork (or similar mixing tool) until the gelatin has completely dissolved.

Step 2

½ cup

2 drops

Next, add ½ cup of corn syrup to the bowl of ingredients—this will add volume and soften the texture of the Ogre Snot. Mix until the consistency is snot-like. The snot will change texture the longer it's played with.

To add some color to the mucus, grab a small vial of food coloring, add a few drops, and mix it in. A typical lowland ogre has yellowish-green mucus (it's a common misperception that they're always sick, but it's just colored enzymes). High-altitude ogres have light blue snot, which is believed to be the strongest healer in the mucus family.

When storing your concoction, remember to tape an Ogre Snot Label (page 225) to the container so no one mistakes it for elderberry jelly.

Step 3

If you're out of gelatin packets, you'll just have to get your Ogre Snot the old-fashioned way! Simply surprise a twelve-foot ogre in his lair and hit him with a sleep spell. Before the ogre reawakes, squeeze as much mucus out of his sneezer and into a jar as possible.

Jar of Fairies

jar

glitter

glow stick

Adult supervision required

Build time
14 minutes

A Jar of Fairies will charm any anxious wizard into a deep sleep. Their small, bug-like wings give off a soothing buzz and a soft magical glow, which is why fairies are often mistaken for fireflies. Coaxing fairy folk into a jar can be difficult, but this lesson teaches you how to catch multiple fairies without a butterfly net or the lure of fruit, muffins, or butter.

Supplies
1 glass jar with twist-off lid
   (or similar see-through
   container)
1 to 4 glow sticks (6 inches
   long each)
1 to 2 tablespoons of glitter

Jar of Fairies Label (page
   226)
Clear tape

Tools
Safety glasses
Scissors

Step 1

activate

Select a glass jar with a twist-off lid. The size of the jar will directly affect the fairy glow: a smaller jar will have less area for the fluorescent dye to cover, creating a more intense glow, while a large jar will be dimmer. Make sure the jar is thoroughly washed and its original label is removed.

Obtain a glow stick and **read its label carefully** for safety instructions and length of glow time. With two hands, active the stick by bending the plastic tube until you hear a snap. When this happens, chemicals in the stick combine to produce light.

Put on safety glasses and position the glow stick over the jar opening. Then, with scissors, cut one end off the plastic housing, letting it fall into the jar. Pour the fluorescent dye into the jar—**being careful not to touch it**, as it can irritate your skin. You may have to cut both ends to pour out all the dye. Additional glow sticks can be added if needed.

Step 2

Pour 1 to 2 tablespoons of glitter into the jar. All shapes and sizes of glitter will work, but superfine iridescent or reflective glitter will produce the best fairies. A larger jar will require more glitter.

Close the jar tightly and shake it. The fine glitter coated in fluorescent dye will stick to the sides of the jar, giving the illusion that glowing fairies are fluttering around inside. For best results, test the captured fairies in a dark room.

Tape a Jar of Fairies Label (page 226) to the side of the jar. You could also paint the jar's lid, or add ribbons or twigs—have fun with it!

Step 3

The grounds of the School of Labcraft Wizards are full of fairies, especially by the road and the gatehouse. They can be lured into the jar with a simple coaxing chant. Fairies are generally harmless but can quickly become agitated when they sense ill intentions. (Although it's frowned upon, some wizards remove fairies' wings for potion ingredients, which tends to displease the fairy community.) To guard against a swarming attack, use a protective charm like a four-leaf clover or wearing your clothes inside out.

Baby Kraken Slime

liquid starch

school glue

water

food coloring

Adult supervision required

Build time
20 minutes

The murky depths of the ocean are home to the fearsome kraken, a gigantic beast whose slimy tentacles crush ships and pull sailors to their doom. Kraken slime offers surprising benefit to the wizard world: it's so magically slimy that it can actually be used to reverse a mild petrification spell! The ooze of full-grown krakens is plentiful but dangerous to harvest, so in this project you'll learn how to obtain a small amount of Baby Kraken Slime.

Supplies

1 full container of clear school glue (~5 fl. oz./150 mL)

Resealable plastic storage bag (large/gallon size)

Water (same amount as glue)

Liquid starch (same amount as glue)

Food coloring (several drops)

Baby Kraken Slime Label (page 227)

Clear tape

Tools

Bowl (optional)

Jar or other airtight container (optional)

Step 1

- - - mix

To produce the Baby Kraken Slime, empty a *full* container of clear school glue into a resealable plastic, gallon-sized storage bag. (White school glue will also work, but clear school glue produces a better slime effect.) The emptied glue container will become the measuring cup for the other ingredients, so pour out as much glue as possible.

Fill the empty glue container to the top with water, then carefully pour that water into the resealable plastic bag. Seal the bag and do some light mixing by pressing both hands into the outside of the bag, squishing the two ingredients together.

Step 2

Fill the empty glue container with liquid starch. Jugs of this product (for instance, Purex Sta-Flo) are available in the school's laundry room, in grocery stores, and online. When the glue container is completely full, carefully pour its contents into the resealable bag.

Last, add a few drops of food coloring to give the slime some color. Depending on the aquatic plants found in the kraken's lair, their slime can be either sickly green, dull beige, or aqua blue. Seal the bag again and do some more mixing by pressing both hands into the sealed bag, squishing all the ingredients together. For a more hands-on mixing experience, you can combine the ingredients in a bowl instead.

Step 3

Baby Kraken Slime is as mysterious as it is magical. You can play with it immediately, but as the mixture sets its texture becomes more interesting. Over several hours, the slime will evolve. Kept in the resealable bag or another airtight container, it will last for weeks. Use tape to affix a Baby Kraken Slime Label (page 227) to the container.

An alternate slime collection method involves a bit of stealth. Adult krakens are found only in the deepest waters, but baby krakens often venture closer to shore. Approach their feeding grounds as quietly as possible, then toss a long rope into the water, with a fish and a large bell tied to the end. Slowly pull in the rope, eventually luring a baby kraken onto the shore. As the kraken crawls toward the bait, the tentacles will leave a slime residue for you to collect.

Bubble Serpent

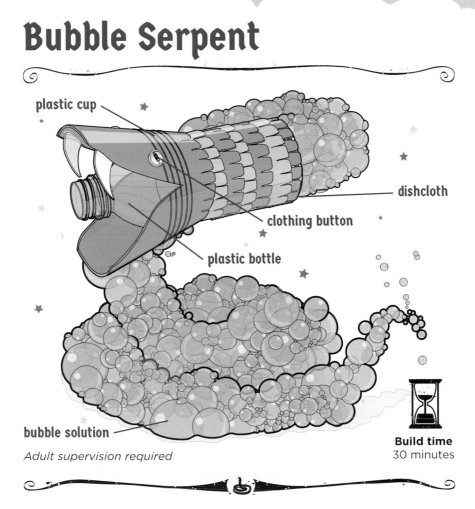

- plastic cup
- dishcloth
- clothing button
- plastic bottle
- bubble solution

Adult supervision required

Build time
30 minutes

One of the most powerful forms of dark magic is the ability to summon dangerous creatures out of thin air. In your final lesson on mythical creatures, you'll learn how to create the dreaded Bubble Serpent, using your own breath to give shape to its slithering form.

Supplies

1 plastic bottle with cap
  (~16.9 fl. oz/500 mL)
1 dishcloth or washcloth
  (at least 4 by 4 inches)
1 rubber band
1 plastic ballpoint pen
3 disposable plastic cups
  (two different colors)
2 white clothing buttons
  (optional)
1 full bottle of bubble
  solution

Tools

Safety glasses
Hobby knife
Scissors
Hot glue gun
Pliers (optional)
Marker (optional)
Bowl

Step 1

Start with a clean, empty plastic bottle (roughly 16.9 fl. oz/500 mL) with an overall diameter of between 2½ and 3 inches. While wearing safety glasses, carefully cut the round plastic base off the bottle with a hobby knife or scissors. Discard the base.

Place the cut bottle onto a dishcloth or washcloth as shown. With scissors, cut a square from the cloth that is ½ inch larger on all sides than the diameter of the bottle. For example, if the bottle diameter is 3 inches, cut a 4-by-4-inch cloth square.

Step 2

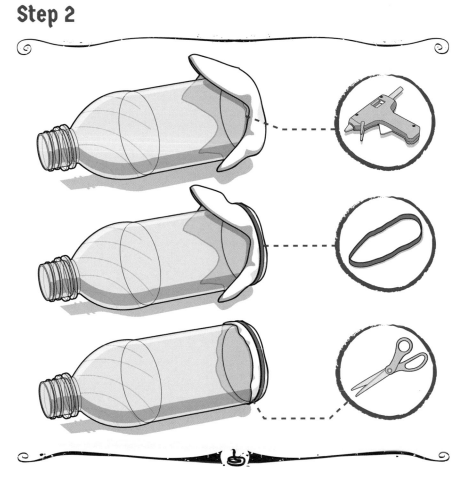

Add hot glue around the large, open end of the bottle and affix the small square cloth over the bottle opening as shown. Place a rubber band around the cloth to keep it secured on the bottle as the hot glue cools.

Next, use scissors to trim any excess cloth behind the rubber band that may be sticking up. Removing this cloth will make it easier to add the optional cup-scales to the bottle.

Step 3

Disassemble a plastic ballpoint pen into its various parts. You may need small pliers to help dislodge the rear pen-housing cap. Next, put on the safety glasses and cut a hole in the plastic bottle's cap with a hobby knife, centered on top of the cap and large enough for the main pen-housing tube to fit through.

Push the hollow pen tube halfway through the bottle cap. Use hot glue to seal the cap in place. Fill in any gaps between the cap and pen housing with glue so the seal is airtight.

Step 4

Optional snake scales can be created out of two disposable cups—two different colors are suggested. To prepare the cups, first use scissors to cut each one down the side, then remove the cups' bottoms and discard them (as shown in the top illustrations). Next, cut each cup into three equal rings. To do this, place the scissors in the existing cut down the side and make small snips while rotating the cup.

Last, add scale details to each ring by clipping out small wedges around the top of each ring as shown. The small incisions will take time, but with some persistence the finished rings will look great on your Bubble Serpent.

Step 5

Time to add the scales to your serpent! Starting at the bottom of the cylinder, hot glue one plastic ring around the bottle. The scaled edge should point away from the top of the bottle and be flush with the attached cloth.

Continue adding scale rings to the bottle, alternating colors if possible. Hot glue each new strip so it overlaps the previous strip, until the scales reach the round bottleneck as illustrated.

Screw in the modified bottle cap with attached pen tube to the top of the bottle.

Step 6

The third disposable cup will become the snake's powerful jaws. Start by removing the bottom of the cup with scissors. Next, shape the upper and lower jaw by cutting out two center wedges as shown, each slightly rounded as it reaches the lip of the cup. Finish the jaw by adding scales to the bottom of the modified cup, using scissors to clip out small wedges as in step 4.

Slide the snake's head onto the top of the bottle, overlapping the other scaled rings. Use hot glue to mount the head in place, slightly below the bottle top so the pen tube protrudes from the snake's mouth.

For additional details, add optional fangs and eyes. For the fangs, cut two curved wedges out of the removed disposable cup bottoms as shown. Use hot glue to mount the fangs to the roof of the mouth. For the eyes, use two white clothing buttons with pupils created with a marker. Mount the buttons onto the side of the head using hot glue.

Step 7

Prepare the ritual to bring the Bubble Serpent to life by dipping the cloth end of the snake into a bowl full of bubble solution. Then take a deep breath, lift the attached pen tube to your lips, and exhale sharply into the bottle. The snake's tail will grow with each puff of air. Challenge friends to see who can create the longest tail.

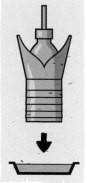

Elemental Charms

Sugar Rainbow

tall glass

water

sugar

Build time
30 minutes

Amaze your wizard classmates by catching a rainbow with the flick of your wand! Although the Sugar Rainbow may seem like an extraordinary feat, it's perfect for your first lesson in elemental charms. This project, which non-magic folk sometimes refer to as a Density Column, requires very few magical components, and when prepared carefully, it will dazzle in the sunlight.

Supplies
1 cup of granulated white sugar
2 cups of water
Food coloring (in 4 different colors)

Tools
4 short drinking glasses

Tablespoon
4 forks
1 tall, narrow drinking glass (or chemistry measuring cylinder)
Plastic syringe (or drinking straw)

Step 1

Dig into the school's glassware collection, locate four short drinking glasses, and line them up on the table.

Add 1 tablespoon of granulated white sugar to the first short glass, 2 tablespoons of sugar to the second glass, 3 tablespoons of sugar to the third glass, and 4 tablespoons of sugar to the fourth glass. When finished, *keep the glasses in order*.

Step 2

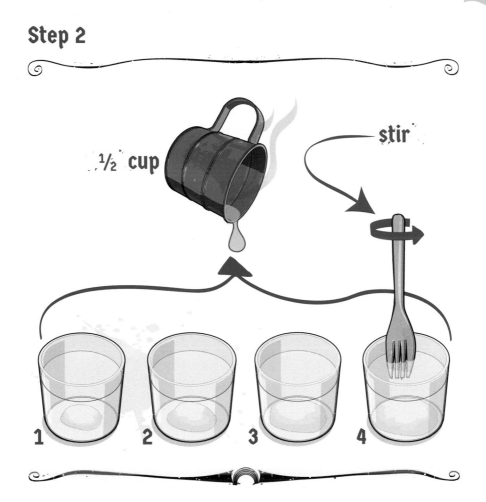

½ cup

stir

1   2   3   4

Next, add ½ cup of water to each of the four glasses. Stir each cup with a fork until the sugar in each is dissolved.

Step 3

4 drops

Time to capture the colors of the rainbow—with the help of some food coloring! Add 4 drops of red coloring to glass 1. Add the same number of drops of yellow to glass 2. In glass 3, add 4 drops of green, and add 4 drops of blue food coloring to glass 4.

Once the drops have been added, use *separate forks* to stir each glass. Using a single fork to mix all four colors could transfer food coloring from glass to glass and muddy the color spectrum.

| 1 | 2 | 3 | 4 |
| RED | YELLOW | GREEN | BLUE |

Step 4

Use a plastic syringe to transfer the blue solution in glass 4 into a tall, narrow drinking glass (or chemistry measuring cylinder). Stop when the tall glass is about one-fourth of the way full.

Clean the syringe, then use it to transfer the green solution in glass 3 onto the top of the blue solution. If it's done carefully, the color layers will stay separate instead of mixing. To keep them from swirling together, release the green solution from the syringe *slowly*, close to the surface of the blue layer, along the side of the tall glass. Add enough green solution to equal the amount of blue.

Continue adding the next two solutions in the same way, washing the syringe before each transfer and releasing the new layer slowly on top of the previous layer. Add the yellow in glass 2 first, then finish with red in glass 1. The colors may bleed together a bit.

No syringe? No problem! Use a drinking straw to slowly transfer the water instead.

Step 5

Behold the power of *density*—the amount of matter contained within a particular unit of space. Each of the short glasses had a different amount of sugar dissolved in the same amount of water; the more sugar that was added, the denser the water became. A less dense water solution will "float" on top of a denser solution, allowing the colored layers to stay separate. Sunlight will amplify their hues.

Frozen Snowstorm

water

glitter

white paint

antacid tablet

baby oil

jar

Adult supervision required

Build time
30 minutes

Even for a wizard, being cooped up inside on cold winter days can be boring. But this simple yet powerful elemental charm can turn a gloomy day into a portable amusement. With a Frozen Snowstorm, you can transport the blustery weather outside into a jar, and keep it gusting indoors as long as you continue to supply the proper ingredients.

Supplies
Large glass jar (or similar see-
     through container)
14 fl. oz. of baby oil
Storm in a Jar Label (page 228)
Clear tape
½ cup of water
1 tablespoon of white craft paint

1 teaspoon of iridescent glitter
     (white, silver, and/or blue)
Effervescent antacid tablets

Tools
Mixing bowl
Fork

Step 1

³/₄ full

Begin this charm by filling a large glass jar with baby oil until it's three-fourths of the way full. You can substitute a similar see-through container, but whatever you use should be at least 5 inches tall for the full snow-gust effect.

Students are encouraged to identify all portable-storm-type elemental charms by taping on a Storm in a Jar Label (page 228).

STORM
IN A JAR

HANDLE
WITH CARE

Step 2

½ cup

1 tablespoon

In a mixing bowl, add ½ cup of warm water. Then add 1 tablespoon of white craft paint to give the water some density and texture.

Step 3

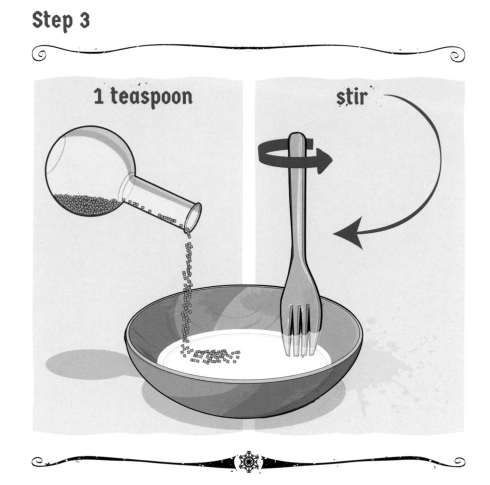

For that sparkling winter effect, add 1 teaspoon of iridescent glitter to the ingredients in the mixing bowl. The wizard faculty suggests that the glitter be in winter colors such as blue, white, and silver. Sparkling glitter snowflakes can also be added.

With a fork (or similar mixing tool), stir up all the ingredients in the mixing bowl until the water turns milky white, with the glitter dispersed throughout.

Step 4

Add the milky-white water to the jar. To avoid a wintry mess on the floor, do not fill the container to the brim. Because the water is denser than the baby oil (see page 90), it will sink to the bottom of the jar.

Once the water mixture has settled, it's time for winter! Add one or more effervescent antacid tablets, such as Alka-Seltzer, to the jar.

Step 5

As the antacid tablets rapidly dissolve, they create bubbles of carbonation that carry the white paint to the surface. Once there, the paint slowly settles back to the bottom of the jar, creating a "storm" cycle. As the bubbles dissipate, add more antacid tablets to keep this winter party going!

Cloud in a Jar

aerosol spray

ice cubes

glass jar

water

Adult supervision required

Build time
20 minutes

Cloud in a Jar has always been a popular practical joke in the wizard world. When opened, it blasts the unsuspecting subject with a sample of severe weather. There are a few different ways of making clouds in a container, but this technique is one of the easiest and most visually stunning.

Supplies
Glass jar with lid
Storm in a Jar Label (page 228)
Clear tape
½ cup of warm water
Ice cubes
Aerosol hair spray or air freshener

Step 1

½ cup

swirl

Locate a glass jar, preferably with its own lid, and designate it for this project by taping on a Storm in a Jar Label (page 228). Pour about ½ cup of warm water into the jar, so there's at least 1 inch of liquid in the bottom. Then swirl around the warm water to heat up the glass. You can also pre-warm the jar by rinsing the inside with warm tap water; you're encouraged to try water at different temperatures to see which produces the best clouds.

Step 2

Turn the jar lid upside down and place several pieces of ice into it. (If your jar is missing its lid, you can substitute a small bowl or plate.) Then place the ice-filled lid on top of the jar. Tilt the cap open just enough to allow you to spray a few spritzes of aerosol hair spray or air freshener into the middle of the jar. Quickly set the iced lid back on top of the jar. Like magic, a cloud will immediately form! (No aerosol? You can use the smoke from a match instead.)

How does the cloud appear? Through the interaction of water vapor, cooling air, and a surface on which to condense. Some of the warm water in the jar is evaporating, and as that water vapor rises, it is cooled by the icy lid. This cooled vapor then condenses onto the tiny particles of the aerosol spray. In the atmosphere, these particles (called *cloud condensation nuclei*) could be smoke, dust, air pollution, sea salt, and more. The cloud movement you see inside the jar is warm air rising and cold air sinking.

Step 3

Cloud in a Jar is the perfect charm to call upon during a wizard duel. The emerging cloud confuses the opponent and cloaks your next attack move!

For best results, release the cloud in direct sunlight or in front of a black backdrop so it stands out more intensely.

Glycerin Smoke

plastic bottle

distilled water

glycerin

tin can

wire hanger

candle

electrical tape

Adult supervision required

Build time
45 minutes

Flabbergast the faculty by learning how to brew magical wisps of smoke that snake into the air. This project will also teach you how to build and use your own versions of common lab equipment such as the Erlenmeyer flask and the Bunsen burner.

Supplies

1 plastic bottle (~16.9 fl. oz./500 mL)
1 small, round tin can (~2.25 oz. with 2½-inch diameter)
Electrical tape or duct tape
1 metal clothes hanger
1 cocktail straw
1 large, round candle (~2½-inch diameter)
½ cup of distilled water
Glycerin (food/high grade)
Match

Tools

Scissors
Hobby knife (optional)
Safety glasses
Can opener with rotating cutter
Wire cutters or diagonal pliers
Plate
Tablespoon
Mixing cup
Fork

Step 1

An ideal container for brewing this charm is an Erlenmeyer flask, notable for its cone-shaped body, flat bottom, and cylindrical neck. This flask is perfect for boiling because the angled sides trap hot vapors. You can create your own Erlenmeyer flask from a modified plastic bottle and small tin can.

Start with an empty plastic bottle approximately 16.9 fl. oz. (500 mL). With scissors or a hobby knife, safety glasses, and an adult's help, cut the round top from the rest of the bottle, as illustrated on the left.

Next, with a rotating can opener, completely remove the top from a small (approximately 2.25 oz.), round tin can, about 2½ inches in diameter and 2½ inches high. An empty can of olives or mushrooms works great. Remove any label and make sure the can is completely clean.

Step 2

With scissors, make several ½-inch vertical cuts around the bottle top's bottom edge. Next, fit the bottle top *over* the tin can opening. The vertical cuts will allow the two parts to slide together; increase the size of the cuts as necessary to create a snug fit. Once they're firmly in place, fasten them together by wrapping electrical tape or duct tape around the assembly as shown.

The flask is finished and looks fantastic! Once you've finished the project with this flask, you can try repeating it with a different flask design to see how it affects the results. Experiment with increasing the flask height, adding the thin spout from the Bubble Serpent (page 78), or removing the bottle neck completely.

Narrow neck   Wide neck   With ground
                              glass joint

Step 3

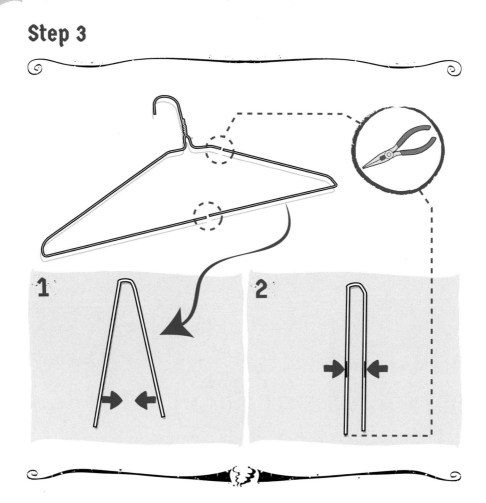

In the next two steps, you'll create a Bunsen burner, a piece of laboratory equipment that produces a single flame for heating. First, obtain a metal clothes hanger, and put on the safety glasses. With a pair of wire cutters or diagonal pliers, make a cut in the center of the lower bar. Then remove one side of the hanger by making a second cut below the twisted neck detail, as shown in the top illustration.

With two hands, slowly bend the metal elbow inward until the two long bars are parallel with one another, approximately ¾ inch apart (see illustrations 1 & 2). With wire cutters, trim the bottom of the bent bars so they are even.

Step 4

With scissors, cut a cocktail straw into three equal parts, each approximately 2 inches long. Slide two of these straw segments over the parallel hanger bars, one per bar. Move both segments all the way up to the hanger elbow.

With electrical tape or duct tape, attach the hanger bar to the side of a large, round candle (roughly 2½-inch diameter). When attached, the metal hanger frame should extend 5 to 8 inches above the top of the candle as shown. The candle will function as the flame of the Bunsen burner.

Step 5

With tape, attach the bottle flask to the two straw segments on the hanger. Tape thoroughly around the full circumference of the flask, as the heat of the burner may weaken the adhesive. Once attached properly, the flask should slide up and down on the hanger rails. This setup is very similar to the adjustable ring stands older students use in their advanced potions lab.

Place the custom chemistry equipment onto a plate, which will protect the work surface from hot wax or spilled liquid.

Step 6

2 tablespoons

1 tablespoon

Pour 2 tablespoons of distilled water into a mixing cup. Then add 1 tablespoon of food-grade or high-grade glycerin, which can be purchased online and in some stores and pharmacies. Spend a few minutes stirring the smoke potion with a fork.

Once you've tried this recipe, you're encouraged to experiment with different ratios of water to glycerin to see how it affects the amount of smoke produced.

Step 7

Add the mixed smoke potion to the bottle flask. Carefully light the candle and use the adjustable ring stand to lower the flask over the flame. After several minutes, smoke will start snaking out of the neck. Command the smoke's movement by waving a magic wand.

2-Liter Tornado

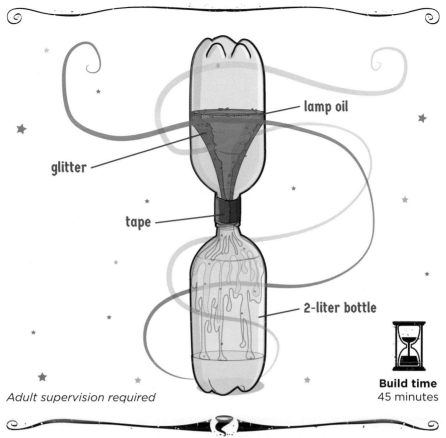

glitter

lamp oil

tape

2-liter bottle

Adult supervision required

Build time
45 minutes

For your last lesson in elemental charms, you'll learn how to summon the swirling winds of a tornado. Tornado charms are difficult to command and can cause a great deal of damage, so for your instructor's sanity, our tiny twisters will be confined to a bottle.

Supplies

2 plastic 2-liter soft drink
　bottles with caps
Superglue or epoxy glue
Water
Colored lamp oil
1 tablespoon of iridescent glit-
　ter (optional)
Duct tape
Storm in a Jar Label (page 228)
Clear tape

Tools

Wooden block
Safety glasses
Hammer
Nail
Phillips head screwdriver
Hobby knife
High grit sandpaper
　(optional)
1 large binder clip (51 mm,
　optional)

Step 1

Start with two plastic 2-liter bottles, emptied and cleaned. Remove the labels and caps from both bottles (illustration 1).

This project will teach you how to manufacture a homemade bottle connector, but vortex bottle connectors can also be purchased online and at toy stores. To create your own connector, place both bottles' caps on a work surface you don't have to worry about scratching or puncturing, such as a wooden block. While wearing safety glasses, and with an adult's help, pound a hole through the center of each cap with a hammer and large nail. Remove the nail (illustration 2).

Next, push the end of a large Phillips head screwdriver or similar tool through the hole to increase the center diameter of both caps. Keep the safety glasses on, and with an adult's help, use a hobby knife to carefully remove any excess material and increase the diameter of the hole (illustration 3).

Step 2

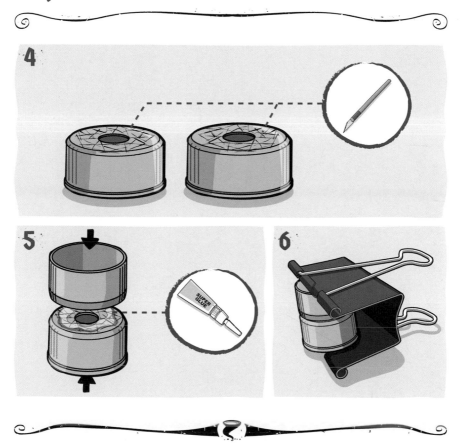

With the hobby knife, scratch and score the smooth top of both plastic bottle caps. You can also use high grit sandpaper; the point is to give the surface some much-needed texture for glue to stick to (illustration 4).

With superglue or epoxy glue, attach the bottle caps to each other, top to top (illustration 5). Optionally, you can use a large binder clip (51 mm) to hold the caps together as they dry (illustration 6). *Make sure the glue does not clog the holes.*

Step 3

Fill one of the 2-liter bottles with tap water until it's one-half to three-fourths of the way full. Add colored lamp oil (citronella torch fuel) to help emphasize the swirling vortex: because oil is less dense then water (see page 90), the colored oil will remain on the top of the water until it spirals down.

Optionally, you can create flying debris by adding 1 tablespoon of iridescent glitter to the bottle. Other debris like bits of Styrofoam can be added as well. Just be mindful of the diameter of the connector hole—don't add anything so big that it will cause clogs. You can also create bubbles by adding a few drops of dish soap.

Step 4

When the top-to-top bottle caps are dry, tightly wrap duct tape around the fixed assembly as an added seal (illustration 7).

Screw the double-cap assembly onto the filled 2-liter bottle (illustration 8). Then screw the empty 2-liter bottle on top. Tightly wrap some additional tape around the bottle necks (illustration 9).

Step 5

To create the vortex, turn the stacked bottles upside down so the full bottle is on top. Use two hands to swirl the bottles clockwise or counterclockwise. Keep rotating until a tornado-like funnel appears.

Once all the liquid has drained into the empty bottle, you can flip them over and go again. Tape a Storm in a Jar Label (page 228) to one or both bottles.

Introduction to Potions

Crystal Courage

corn syrup

cream of tartar

COURAGE

sugar

food coloring

water

Build time
1½ to 3½ hours

Adult supervision required

Crystal Courage—which those unfamiliar with its magical properties might simply call Candy Glass—is a powerful potion that gives anyone who consumes it a quick surge of energy to help overcome difficult challenges.

Supplies
Aluminum foil
1 cup of water
3½ cups of granulated white
    sugar
1 cup of light corn syrup
¼ teaspoon of cream of tartar
Food coloring (optional)
Flavored gelatin (optional)
Crystal Courage Label (page 229)
Clear tape

Tools
Large cookie sheet
Heavy nonstick saucepan
Silicone spatula
Candy thermometer
Hot pads or oven mitts
Towel
Hammer or other smashing
    tool

Step 1

Cover a large cookie sheet with raised sides with aluminum foil. The overall size of the cookie sheet and the height of the sides depends on how large a batch of Crystal Courage you'd like to make. Parchment paper or cooking spray can be substituted for aluminum foil—but be aware that some cooking sprays will affect the taste of the sugar.

Step 2

1 cup

3½ cups

In a heavy nonstick saucepan or fortified cauldron, stir together 1 cup of water and 3½ cups of granulated white sugar (table sugar). When heated later in the project, the sugar mixture could boil up, so use a deep pan. A silicone spatula is recommended for mixing, especially in the later steps, because it is easier to clean.

Step 3

1 cup
¼ teaspoon

Next, mix in 1 cup of light corn syrup and ¼ teaspoon of cream of tartar. *Light* corn syrup is recommended because otherwise the finished Crystal Courage will turn out too dark.

Step 4

stir

low heat

Once you have the right ingredients added, you can begin to brew Crystal Courage. You'll use the stove, **which should always be done with caution and adult supervision**. Slowly bring the ingredients to a boil over low or medium heat. Low heat will reduce the chance of browning. Stir the ingredients continually with the silicone spatula so you don't scorch the bottom of the pan. **Never leave ingredients unattended on the burner.**

Step 5

(300°F)

25 to 60 minutes

Use a candy thermometer to determine when the mixture has reached 300°F; this could take anywhere from 25 to 60 minutes. At this temperature, the mixture enters what is known as the "hard crack" phase and develops a syrup-like consistency, and is ready to be removed. At this point, you may wish to quickly add a few drops of food coloring and a pinch of flavored gelatin to the mix. Quickly stir in any added ingredients, then turn off the burner and carefully remove the saucepan from the stove with hot pads or oven mitts.

Step 6

1 to 2 hours

Holding the pan with the hot pads or oven mitts, **carefully and slowly** pour the hot sugar mixture onto the prepared cookie sheet from step 1. Pouring in a thin stream 1 to 2 feet above the sheet will help eliminate air bubbles. Evenly disperse the candy by trying to fill the entire cookie sheet.

 Be careful! The heated sugar syrup is extremely hot and will stick to skin if spilled. **Adult supervision is a must.**

Once the mixture is poured, leave the cookie sheet to cool at room temperature until the candy is completely hardened. It could harden in as quickly as 30 minutes, but it's safest to wait 1 to 2 hours. Do not try to speed up the hardening process by placing the cooling pan in the freezer or refrigerator, as this could cause the candy to shatter unexpectedly.

Step 7

A simple smashing spell can shatter the cooled Crystal Courage, but we encourage something more hands-on: place a clean towel over the cooled mixture, then hit it gently with a hammer or another blunt object to break the glass! Keep hitting in several places until the glass is bite size. Place in a small container and tape a Crystal Courage Label to it (page 229), so you know just what to reach for whenever you need a quick burst of bravery.

Wizard's Tree

cardboard

food coloring

table salt

water

ammonia

Mrs. Stewart's Bluing

Adult supervision required

Build time
1 to 3 days

Some of the world's most powerful magic wands are crafted from special trees grown by the wizards of ages past, centuries-old wood laced with ancient magic. In this lesson, novice wizards will learn how to mix up a potion capable of growing their own miniature version of a Wizard's Tree. With a drop of this and a pinch of that, you can conjure up a unique colored tree in only few days!

Supplies

1 thick, corrugated cardboard box (at least 8 by 6 inches on one side)
Food coloring (a few drops)
1 tablespoon of table salt
1 tablespoon of water
1 tablespoon of Mrs. Stewart's Bluing

½ tablespoon of ammonia

Tools

Marker or pen
Ruler
Scissors
Small bowl (~5-inch diameter)
Tablespoon

Step 1

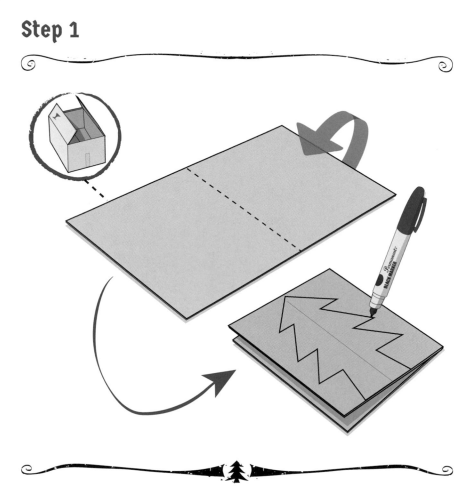

Start with an empty cardboard box made from thick, corrugated cardboard. With a ruler and a marker or pen, measure out an 8-by-6-inch rectangle on one of the sides. Cut out the rectangle with scissors.

Fold the rectangle in half, creating a 4-by-6-inch double-walled rectangle. Then, with a marker, draw a simple silhouette of a tree. The illustration shows a pine tree created out of basic triangles that is easy to cut out and assemble. Other possible tree shapes are shown below.

Step 2

Use the scissors to cut the tree shape out of both sides of the folded cardboard sheet, creating two identical tree patterns (top).

Place the two tree patterns side by side. On the centerline of the first tree, use the scissors to cut a small slit from the top of the tree to about halfway down, as shown (bottom). On the center of the second tree pattern, cut a small slit from the bottom edge to approximately halfway up the tree. Both slits' widths should be equal to the thickness of the cardboard.

Step 3

Slide the two trees patterns together to create a single three-dimensional tree that can stand unassisted.

To add color to the Wizard Tree, add a few drops of food coloring to the edges, letting the dye soak into the cardboard. Without the dye, the Wizard Tree will grow white—which is also perfectly fine.

Step 4

1 tablespoon

1 tablespoon

In a small bowl (roughly 5-inch diameter), pour 1 tablespoon of table salt (iodized or plain) and 1 tablespoon of water.

Step 5

1 tablespoon

BLUING

LIQUID

In the same bowl, add 1 tablespoon of Mrs. Stewart's Bluing, which can be purchased online and at many grocery stores. The solution is nontoxic but should be handled with care and adult supervision. ***Read the manufacturer's label before using.***

Step 6

½ tablespoon

24 to 48 hours

To finish the potion, add ½ tablespoon of household ammonia. Make sure the ammonia container is properly sealed when finished. ***Do not breathe the fumes.***

Stand the cardboard tree upright in the center of the bowl and wait for the potion to take effect! Within 24 hours, colorful foliage will start to grow up the side of the Wizard's Tree. To increase the size of the tree, as the potion disappears over the next several days, replenish it with more of the same mixture.

Step 7

The cardboard tree soaks up the potion, similar to how a process called *capillary action* draws water up from the roots of a real tree. When the solution reaches the edges of the cardboard tree, it mixes with the food coloring soaked into the limbs and begins to evaporate; the added ammonia helps speed up this evaporation. When the potion evaporates, the salt and the blue iron particles in the bluing are left behind, as is the food coloring, creating colorful crystal leaves.

Magic Sand

drinking glass

water

sand

waterproofing spray

Build time
1 day

Novice wizards are introduced to all kinds of spells and potions, but one of their favorites is Magic Sand. When properly brewed, this potion renders simple beach sand immune to the effects of water—allowing it to emerge completely dry when soaked. It's a surprisingly simple inanimate defense potion and a must-try for all students.

Supplies
Aluminum foil
1 cup of sand
Waterproofing spray (such as
    Scotchgard)
Water

Tools
Cookie sheet
Drinking glass (or similar
    container)

Step 1

1 CUP

Create a work surface by covering a cookie sheet with aluminum foil. Make sure to wrap the foil around the edges to completely protect the tray. You can substitute a different work surface, such as a large piece of cardboard—anything that is either protected or disposable, and that you can shake to spread out the sand in the steps to come. Keep in mind that a large work surface will allow you to prepare the sand more quickly.

Pour one cup of dried sand onto the cookie sheet. Beach sand, sandbox sand, or sand from the pet store all work just fine. Once the sand is poured, gently shake the sheet to spread out the sand evenly.

Step 2

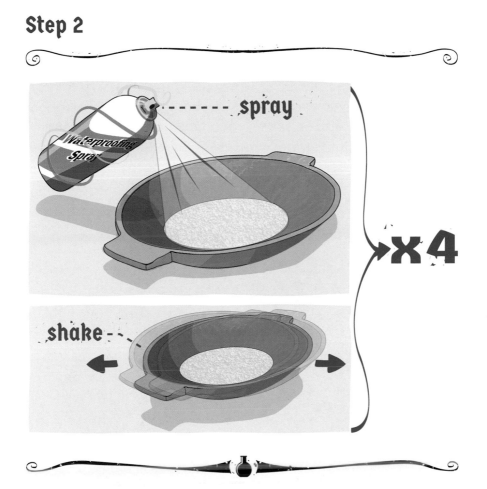

Spray an even coat of Scotchgard or similar waterproofing spray over the top of the sand. Once the sand has dried (see the product label for recommended drying time), do a light shake to expose untreated surfaces and apply the spray again. Repeat this step a few more times.

After a few coats have been applied, the sand has been made *hydrophobic*—it repels water, similar to how vegetable oil repels water. In fact, the waterproofing spray basically adds a permanent coating of oil around each piece of sand. (The opposite of hydrophobic is *hydrophilic*; a good example of a hydrophilic substance is food coloring, which mixes with water.)

Step 3

Test the potion's results by slowly pouring the Magic Sand into a glass of water. If you look closely, you should see small silver bubbles forming around the sand—a good indication that the elixir is working! Pour out the water or use a spoon to scoop out the sand; the sand should be dry to the touch!

Hot Ice

baking soda

vinegar

Adult supervision required

Hot Ice is one of the most advanced potions novice wizards will attempt. It uses common ingredients to create *sodium acetate*, a mysterious substance that transforms from a liquid into icy crystals at room temperature. This is a complicated potion to brew that even elder wizards struggle to perfect.

Supplies
4¼ cups of vinegar
4 tablespoons of baking soda
4 cups of water (optional)
4 cups of ice cubes (optional)

Tools
Large cooking pot
Hot pads or oven mitts
Bowl with lid
Casserole dish or other large
    container (optional)

Step 1

4¼ cups

4 tablespoons

BAKING SODA

Add 4¼ cups of vinegar to a large cooking pot or fortified cauldron. Then gradually add 4 tablespoons of baking soda while stirring. If the baking soda is added too quickly, the vinegar and the baking soda will quickly react with each other to create carbon dioxide and bubble over the sides of the cooking pot.

Step 2

30 to 60 minutes

medium heat

At this point the ingredients in the pot have combined to create sodium acetate, but the potion is currently too diluted by water to be very powerful. You'll need to boil the solution to remove the extra water. **With an adult's supervision**, place the pot onto medium heat for anywhere from 30 to 60 minutes. **Do not leave the boiling material unattended.**

Step 3

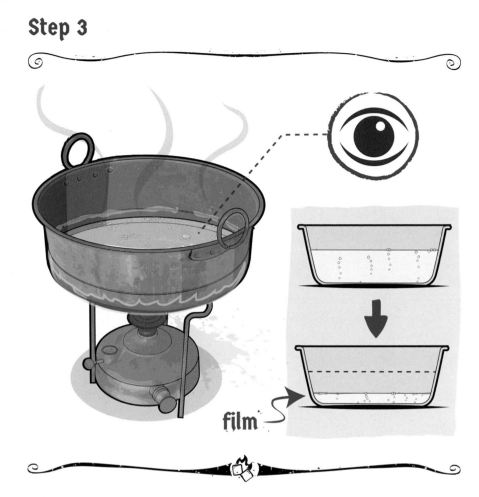

film

Allow the potion to boil down to approximately one-fourth of its original depth. Around this point, observe the surface closely; the potion will be ready when visible film or crystal skin starts to form on the boiling surface. At the first trace of film, remove the pot from the heat with hot pads or oven mitts.

Step 4

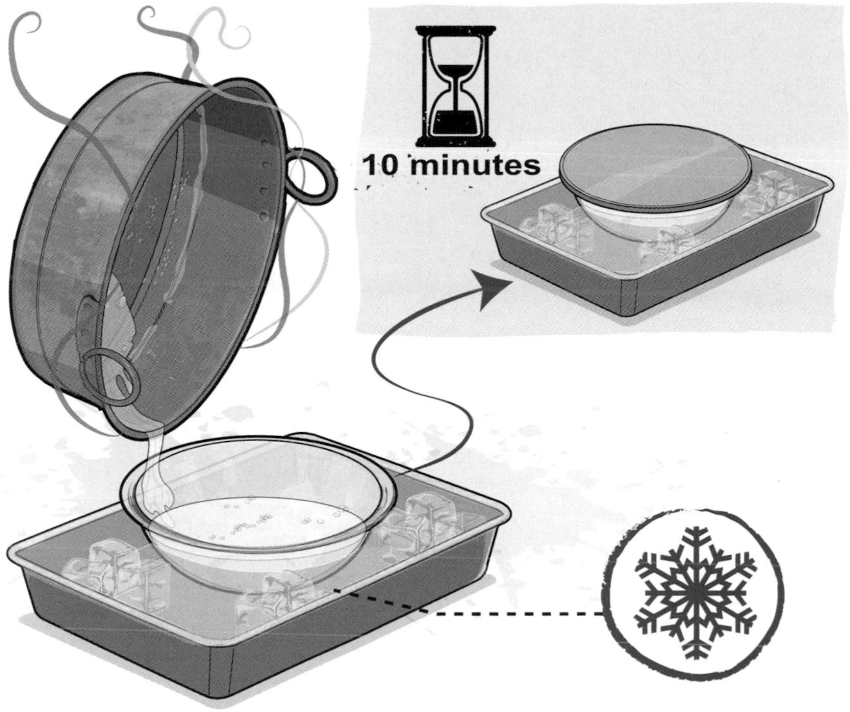

10 minutes

Pour the solution into a separate bowl with a lid and immediately cover the container to prevent any foreign objects from getting into the potion and activating it prematurely. Check the empty pot and save any visible crystals that might have formed around the edge. These are crystals of sodium acetate, which can be used in step 5 to create the "ice" reaction.

Cool the Hot Ice by placing the bowl in the refrigerator, or in a casserole dish or other container large enough to hold the bowl, 4 cups of water, and 4 cups of ice cubes, as illustrated above. Leave the potion in the refrigerator or icy water for at least 10 minutes to allow it to cool.

Once cooled, the sodium acetate will be actually be *super-cooled*, meaning it will stay in liquid form even though it's below its usual freezing point.

Step 5

Because the solution is below its usual freezing point, the right conditions will cause it to spontaneously solidify. Just sprinkle a pinch of baking soda or a few leftover sodium acetate crystals from step 4 into the liquid, and it will crystallize on command. This reaction is *exothermic*, which means it will also generate heat.

To create an icy tower like the one shown on page 137, place a crystal of sodium acetate or a pinch of baking soda in the center of an empty dish, slowly pour the cooled sodium acetate liquid on top of the crystal, and watch it grow.

Cerebral Stone

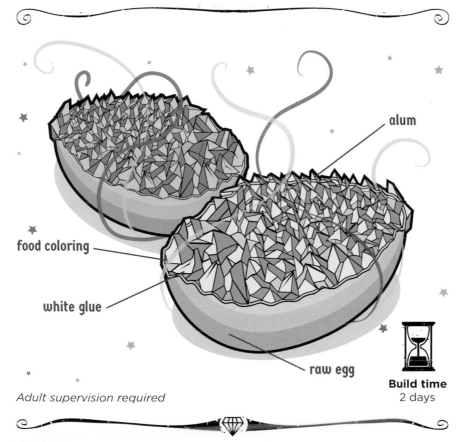

alum

food coloring

white glue

raw egg

Adult supervision required

Build time
2 days

Enchanted stones are among the most convenient magical vessels in the wizard world. They allow a spellcaster to carry anything from a simple protection spell to the secret to eternal life in the palm of his or her hand. In this lesson, you'll learn the potion used to create a Cerebral Stone. Known among the non-magical as Crystal Geodes, they're carried by wizards to improve their mental focus and magical concentration.

Supplies
1 raw egg
Drinking straw
Paper towels
White glue
1 cup of powdered alum
1 to 2 cups of hot water
Food coloring

Tools
Plate
Small hobby paintbrush
Small scissors
Drinking glass (or similar container)
Spoon
Microwave (optional)

Step 1

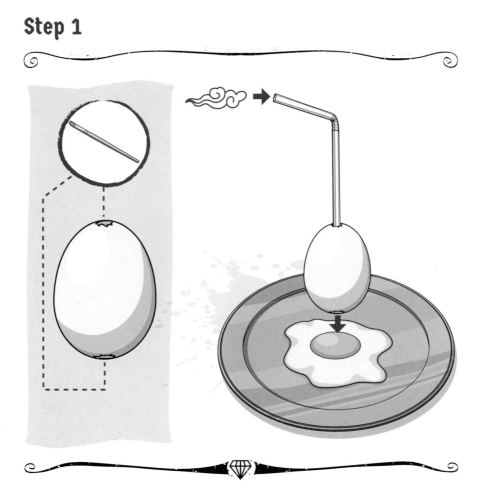

The first step to creating the Cerebral Stone is emptying the contents of one raw egg—chicken, snake, or dragon. To prevent a mess, hold the egg over a plate. Then, with the blunt end of a small hobby paintbrush, poke one hole through the top of the eggshell and another small hole in the bottom of the eggshell.

Insert a drinking straw into the top eggshell hole. Place your lips to the straw and blow several times to flush out the raw egg. Throw away the raw egg and straw and clean your hands thoroughly.

Step 2

Under a running faucet, rinse out the hollow eggshell by flushing water over and through the openings.

Insert the tip of a small pair of scissors into one of eggshell holes, and carefully cut the eggshell in half, lengthwise, as shown. If needed, use additional running water to clean the inside of the shell.

Step 3

dry first

GLUE Multi-Purpose

Alum

24 hours

With a paper towel, carefully dry the inside of both halved egg-shells. Next, with the small paintbrush, apply an even coat of white glue to the inside of the each eggshell and around the broken shell edges (left). Rinse off the paintbrush when you're done.

Sprinkle powdered alum onto the wet glue covering the egg-shell until the shell is completely covered with an even coat of alum. Let the glue dry; this may take up to 24 hours.

Step 4

2 cups   **¾ cup**

Find a small drinking glass (or bowl or other container) that has a bottom that can fit one or two eggshells.

Add 1 to 2 cups of hot water (almost boiling) to the glass. Then use a spoon to stir in ¾ cup of powdered alum. The water temperature and stirring will help the powder to dissolve completely. If some alum particles are still visible, place the solution into the microwave for a few minutes to increase the water temperature.

Step 5

20 drops

Let the solution cool for about 20 minutes. During this time, add 20 drops of food coloring to the solution. Use the spoon to mix it in.

If you wish to make several different colored Cerebral Stones, use multiple containers.

Step 6

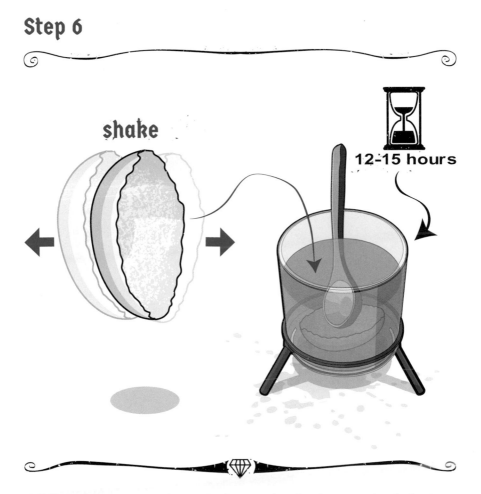

shake

12-15 hours

With the alum-coated eggshell completely dry, gently shake it to remove any excess powder that isn't stuck to the shell. Using the spoon, submerge the eggshell in the hot water solution with the inside facing up. Allow the shell to remain undisturbed for 12 to 15 hours.

As the solution cools, it won't be able to hold as much dissolved material, and floating alum particles will appear. These particles will begin to settle onto the alum covering the eggshell, a process called *sedimentation*. As time passes, more and more sedimentation will occur, and the alum particles will link together to form larger and larger crystals. Crystals may also appear on the bottom of the glass.

Cerebral Stone

Step 7

After 12 to 15 hours, check the eggshells for crystal growth. Once you see crystal growth of ¼ to ½ inch, use the spoon to retrieve the transformed eggshells and place them onto a paper towel or drying rack. The newly formed crystals will be fragile until they dry.

The completed Cerebral Stone resembles a rock formation known as a *geode*. Geodes are hollow rocks in which crystals have grown through a similar chemical process to the one that transformed the eggshells.

Brew Slugs

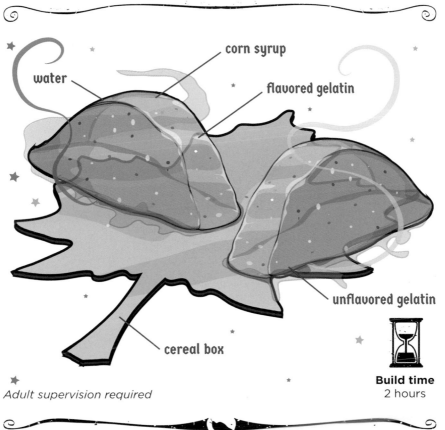

water

corn syrup

flavored gelatin

unflavored gelatin

cereal box

Adult supervision required

Build time
2 hours

Conjuring up a flock of birds or a swarm of bees is beyond a novice wizard's power, but in your final potions lesson, you'll learn how to brew up a batch of simpler life-forms: small, slimy slugs. Not only can they be crafted from common ingredients, but in a hilariously disgusting twist, they're edible, too!

Supplies

½ cup of cold water
¼ cup of corn syrup
2 unflavored gelatin packets
   (0.25 oz. each)
1 box of flavored gelatin (3 oz.)
Vegetable oil
1 empty cereal box
Edible Slugs Label (page 230)
Clear tape

Tools

Mixing cup
Fork
Medium-sized cooking pot
Hot pads or oven mitts
Cupcake pan
Knife
Scissors

Step 1

First, measure ½ cup of cold water and ¼ cup of corn syrup, and add both to a mixing cup. Stir the ingredients with a fork until mixed thoroughly—no lumps or clumps should be visible. At this point, the corn syrup is fully dissolved.

Step 2

add mix

2 packets

Gelatin

UNFLAVORED

Pour your mixture into a medium-sized cooking pot—but do not place the pot on the stove yet. First, grab two packs of unflavored gelatin (0.25 oz. each), and sprinkle both packets into the pot. Gelatin does not dissolve easily in cold water, so some slight mixing will help. This added gelatin will give the slugs a soft, organic feel.

Step 3

Dump an entire 3 oz. box of flavored gelatin dessert (such as Jell-O) into the pot. Slugs come in a variety of colors. See the slug chart below to help identify the "flavor" of each slug.

Slowly stir the added gelatin until the powder is completely dissolved.

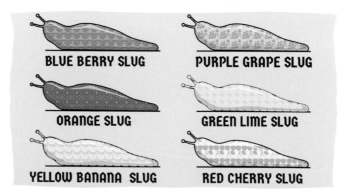

BLUE BERRY SLUG	PURPLE GRAPE SLUG
ORANGE SLUG	GREEN LIME SLUG
YELLOW BANANA SLUG	RED CHERRY SLUG

Step 4

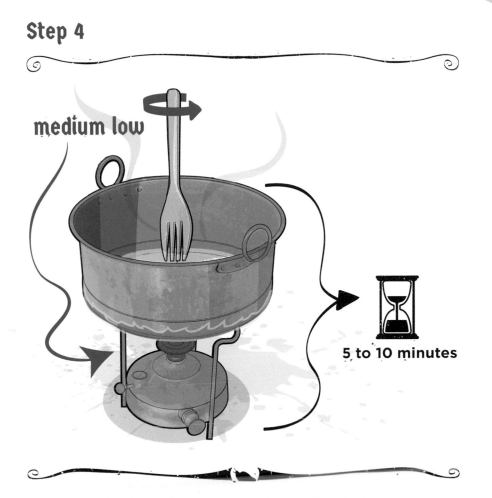

medium low

5 to 10 minutes

Transform the ingredients into a slug potion before your very eyes by placing the cooking pot on the stove with the heat set at medium low. Let the ingredients cook for 5 to 10 minutes to melt the gelatin, stirring regularly to avoid burnt slug goo.

When the gelatin appears to be melted and liquefied, turn off the burner and use hot pads or oven mitts to carefully remove the pot from the stove.

Step 5

coat pan

You will use a cupcake pan to create the slug bodies. To keep the mixture from sticking to the pan, first add a light coat of vegetable oil to each individual cup. (No oil is necessary if your cupcake pan is nonstick.)

Pour a small amount of the hot, sluggy syrup into each cup—around ½ inch of mix per circle. The number of molds you can fill will depend on the amount of liquid and the size of the cups. Each cup will produce two half-circle gummy slugs.

Step 6

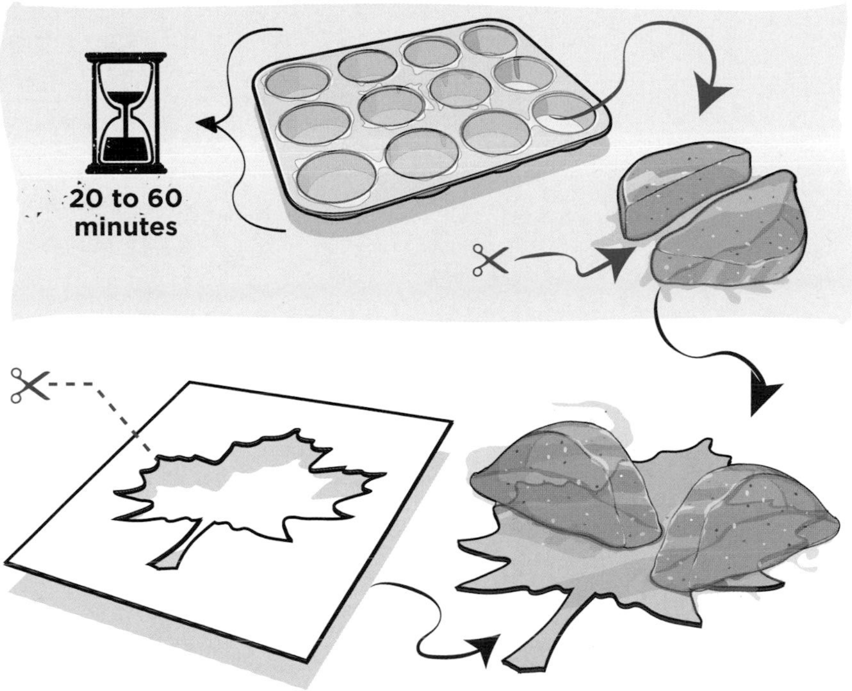

Let the flavored slugs cool for about 20 to 60 minutes (putting them in the fridge will reduce cooling time), or until the gelatin has solidified and is cool to the touch. Remove the round gelatin circles from the pan. (If you want an extra-gross eating experience, you can remove the circles from the pan a bit prematurely for a slimy feel!)

Use a knife to cut each gummy circle in half. Then place the cut circles flat side down for a round, jiggly slug.

For a fun way to consume your creations, cut out a few leaf serving trays from an empty cereal box. First, draw a simple leaf shape similar to the illustration above, and then use scissors to remove the pattern. Load the leaf with tasty slugs and serve.

Step 7

If you have any leftover slugs, place them in a container and tape on an Edible Slugs Label (page 230). Store them in the refrigerator until the next time you get the urge for a cold, slimy snack!

Enchantments

Memory Cell

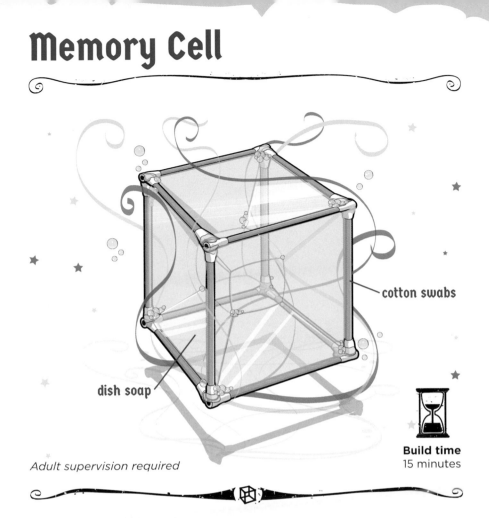

cotton swabs

dish soap

Adult supervision required

Build time
15 minutes

The Memory Cell is designed to steal a specific memory from an unsuspecting victim and then erase it. For such fiendish magic, its construction is quite simple, requiring only a handful of cotton swabs. The hard part is deciding what circumstances call for unleashing its fearsome power.

Supplies
12 plastic cotton swabs
Dish soap

Tools
Scissors
Hot glue gun
Bowl

Step 1

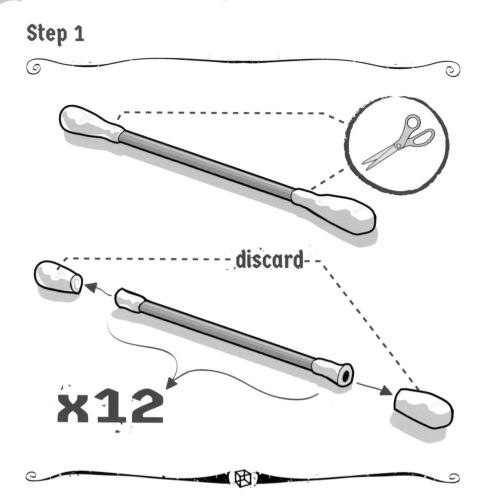

discard

x12

Locate 12 cotton swabs. Experienced wizards recommend plastic-stemmed swabs for their durability. Traditional soft-shaft swabs will deteriorate with use, eventually rendering the Memory Cell useless. (Plastic pipettes can also be substituted, cut and/or bent into a frame similar to the one in step 2, with each side about 4 inches long.)

With scissors, carefully remove both cotton ends from each of the cotton swabs. Discard the removed cotton ends; they will not be used.

Step 2

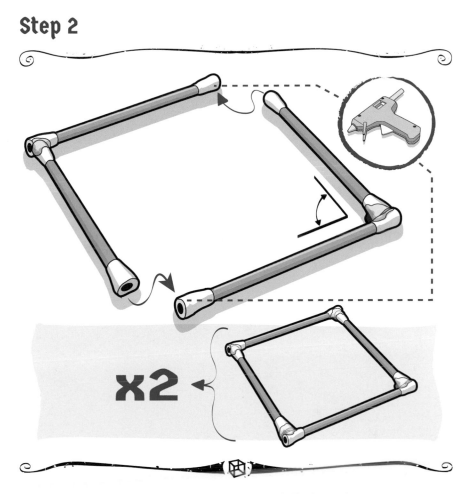

x2

Begin assembly of the cube by carefully hot gluing two cotton swab ends together, positioned at a 90-degree angle as shown. Allow the glue to set. Create three more identical 90-degree pairs.

Take two of the 90-degree pairs and hot glue them together to make a square. Create one more square using the two remaining cotton swab pairs. You have now completed two faces of the Memory Cell cube.

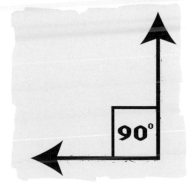

90°

Step 3

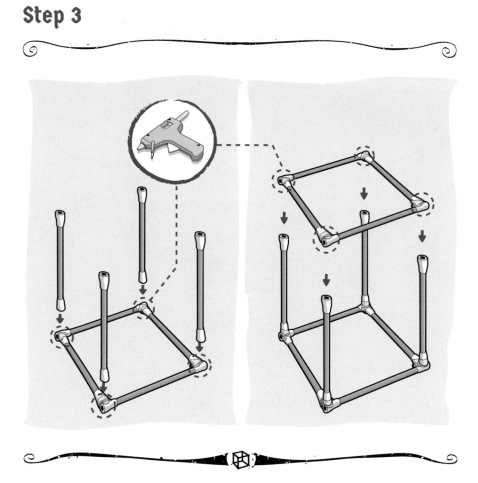

Place one of the completed squares on a flat surface. Hot glue the four remaining swabs vertically onto the four corners of the square, as indicated in the left illustration. Do your best to make sure the newly attached swabs stand straight up, at a 90-degree angle. Allow the glue to cool.

Finish constructing the cube by hot gluing the second square on top the four newly attached vertical swabs, as shown in the right illustration. Let the finished cube assembly dry. If the cube seems wobbly, add additional hot glue to all the cube corners to strengthen the structure.

Step 4

Find a shallow bowl into which the finished Memory Cell can fit, as shown in the top left illustration. You will also need to locate dish soap, which may be difficult because of the effectiveness of self-cleaning spells.

Add the dish soap to the bowl, approximately ½ inch deep, or enough to completely submerge one face of the Memory Cell. (In a larger container, you can submerge every face of the cube at once, but that will require a lot more soap.)

Step 5

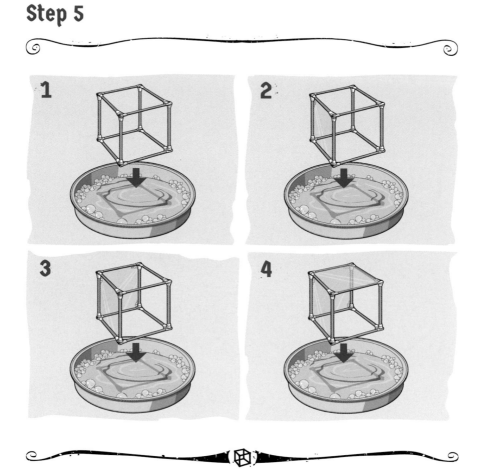

With one hand, grab two upper corners of the Memory Cell, then submerge the bottom face of the cube in the enchanted bubbles (illustration 1). Slowly remove the submerged face from the bowl, and rotate the Memory Cell to dip another face in the soap. An intact bubble wall should still be clinging to the first side you submerged (illustration 2).

Carefully rotate the Memory Cell again and dip a third face in the soap, making sure not to pop any of the existing bubble walls (illustration 3). Continue to add bubble walls to all six sides have been completed (illustration 4).

Step 6

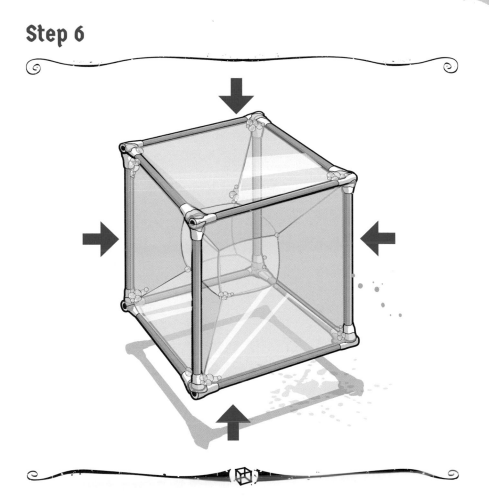

With bubble walls clinging to all six sides, the Memory Cell is ready to use! Force will pull the square bubble walls inward, creating a miniature cube suspended within the constructed frame. If no mini bubble cube appears, gently jiggle the frame or blow softly on the bubble walls to encourage it to form.

Step 7

Don't gaze upon the Memory Cell's dark beauty for too long; the door to the cell will only stay intact for a few minutes. With magic wand in hand, recite the Memory Cell spell, imprisoning the captured thought until it's discarded with a "*pop!*":

Wizards beware, once this spell is spoken,
And once the Memory Cell is broken,
The memory can't be reawoken.

Bubble Mirror

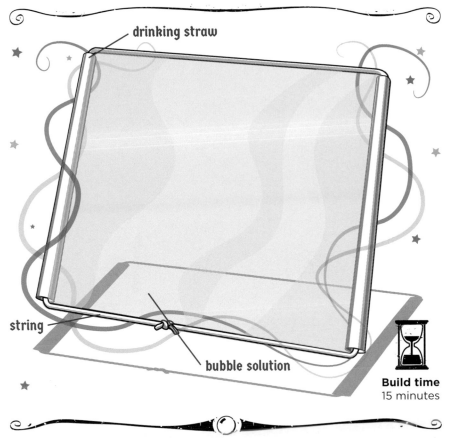

drinking straw

string

bubble solution

Build time
15 minutes

The Bubble Mirror is a handheld device used by wizards to uncover any hidden magical influences on themselves or the world around them. This enchanted artifact can be created quickly, and awoken simply by immersing it in bubble solution. While student spell-casters rarely need to worry about lurking magical threats, they do enjoy the shimmering images and floating shapes the mirror reveals.

Supplies

1 gallon of water
⅔ cup of dish soap
1 tablespoon of glycerin
2 drinking straws
24 to 30 inches of craft string
    or yarn

Tools

Large baking pan
Scissors

Step 1

1 gallon   ⅔ cup   1 tablespoon

To hold enough bubble solution to power the Bubble Mirror, you'll need a large baking pan. It should be at least 16 inches by 14 inches, with raised sides to prevent the solution from spilling out.

You can fill the pan with regular bubble solution if you have about 1 gallon on hand, but if you don't have enough, it's easy to create your own. Pour 1 gallon of water into the baking pan. (Distilled water is the best, but tap water will work just fine.) Then add ⅔ cup of dish soap and about 1 tablespoon of glycerin. Glycerin can be found online and at most pharmacies. Gently stir the ingredients together for a potion that should produce very big bubbles.

Step 2

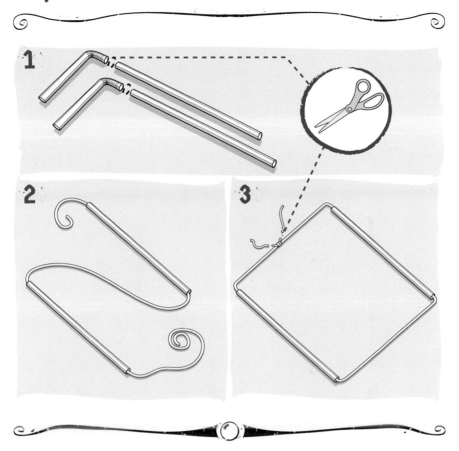

Now construct a mirror frame from two drinking straws. If the straws have flexible heads, use scissors to cut them off, just below the bendable sections (illustration 1).

Run approximately 24 to 30 inches of craft string or yarn through both modified drinking straws (illustration 2). Tie the ends together and trim off any extra string (illustration 3). Slide the attached straws to either side, creating a string-straw rectangle.

You can also experiment with larger mirror frames. The string segment can be as long as eight times the height of one straw.

Step 3

The Bubble Mirror reveals the potential for big laughs and giant bubbles! Outside, dip the two drinking straws into the bubble liquid and carefully remove them, stretching them apart to create a rectangular window covered with bubble film. Gaze into the bubble window, or increase the size of the bubble by sliding the mirror across the sky.

Dancing Candle

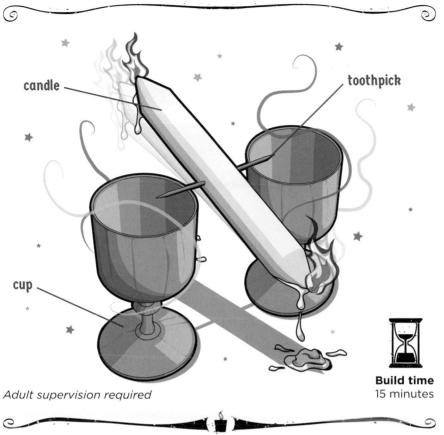

candle

toothpick

cup

Adult supervision required

Build time
15 minutes

The Dancing Candle enchantment, also known as Seesaw Candle or Dueling Candles, is popular with novice wizards because it only takes a few minutes to master. Once the two-headed candle is activated, it will dance without rest, until both candlewicks neither flicker nor flare.

Supplies

1 taper/dinner candle (6 to 18 inches long)

2 round toothpicks, or 1 long needle or metal clothes hanger

2 tall cups

Aluminum foil (or other fire-safe surface)

Matches

Tools

Safety glasses

Hobby knife

Wire cutters or diagonal pliers (optional)

Needle-nose pliers (optional)

Step 1

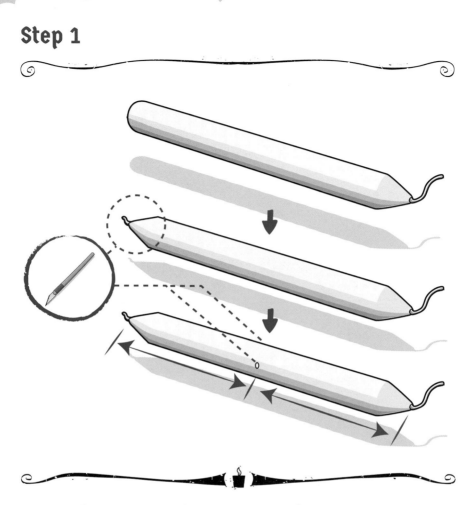

Start with one 6- to 18-inch-long taper/dinner candle (see the different candle types below). The candle's diameter should be around ¾ to 1 inch. Put on safety glasses and use a hobby knife or similar cutting tool to remove the wax from the flat end of the candle until this end is tapered to match the opposite end, exposing the wick, as shown in the middle illustration.

Next, use the hobby knife to make two small indentations at the candle's center point, directly across from one another on opposite sides of the candle, as shown in the bottom illustration.

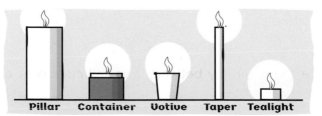

Step 2

You'll anchor the candle with a center bar, which can be fixed to the candle in several different ways. Whichever method you choose, keep wearing the safety glasses in case the center bar slips. The easiest way is to push two round toothpicks into the side of the candle, using the two small indentations as guides. Both toothpicks should be pushed firmly into the wax—but not all the way through it.

A trickier but sturdier method is to use a long needle, or a segment cut from a metal clothes hanger with wire cutters or diagonal pliers. Hold the metal item with needle-nose pliers or a similar tool and use a match to heat the end, and you'll be able to push it through the candle with ease.

Balance the assembly between two tall cups over a sheet of aluminum foil or another fire-safe surface, such as a metal cookie sheet or a large porcelain serving dish, as shown on the right.

Step 3

Carefully light both ends and watch as they dance up and down! The movement is caused by the constantly changing balance between the candle ends. Whichever flame is lower will burn off wax faster, eventually causing the lower end to become lighter and switch positions. This back-and-forth movement will continue until both ends burn down.

Stacking Water

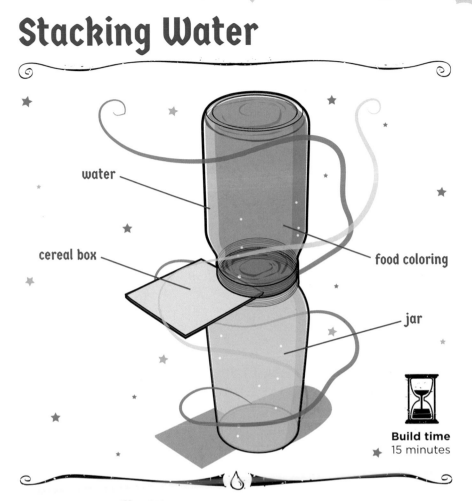

water

cereal box

food coloring

jar

Build time
15 minutes

"Hocus-no-spillus!" Harnessing the powers of heat and cold, the Stacking Water enchantment temporarily prevents two stacked vessels of water from mixing together. Setup is quick and easy, requiring only a few common items from the potions pantry. Just don't turn away—restrained only by the differing properties of hot and cold water, this enchantment will lose its hold once their temperatures equalize.

Supplies
2 identical jars (or similar identical containers)
Warm water
Food coloring (a few drops)
Cold water
1 empty cereal box (or similar piece of cardboard)

Tools
Scissors

Step 1

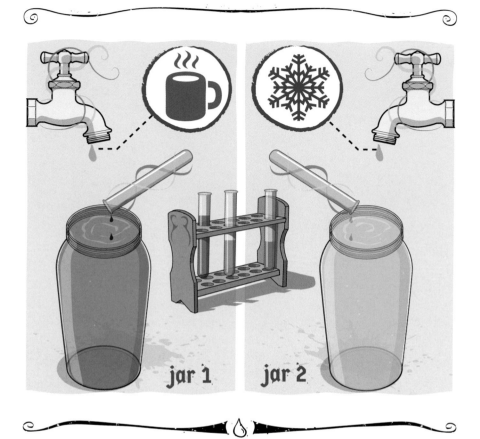

jar 1   jar 2

To get started, locate two identical jars. Containers other than jars can be used as well, as long as both are exactly the same. Fill the first jar to the brim with warm water, and add a few drops of food coloring to give it color. Then fill the second jar to the brim with cold water. Add food coloring to this jar, too—a different color than in the first jar.

You may notice that the food coloring disperses more quickly in warm water than in cold. This is because the molecules of warm water are moving around faster, making it easier for them to interact with the particles of dye. The faster motion also makes warm water less *dense* than cold water, meaning there are fewer molecules of water in the same amount of space. This difference in density is what powers the Stacking Water enchantment.

Step 2

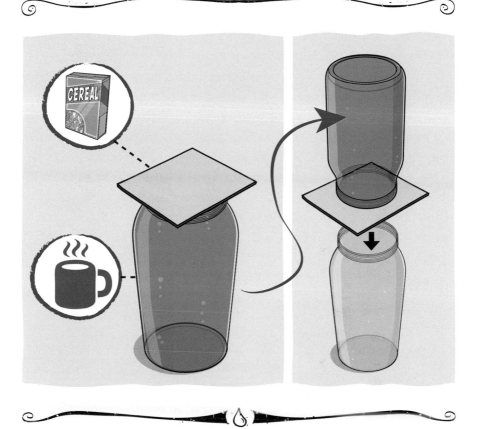

With scissors, remove a square from an empty cereal box (or similar source of cardboard), big enough to completely cover the jar openings. Place it on top of the open jar full of warm water as a temporary seal (left).

This rest of the project should be done over a sink or outside, where it's OK if things get wet. Holding both the warm jar and the attached cardboard cover, quickly turn the warm jar upside down and place it on top of the cold jar.

Step 3

With the cardboard square still dividing both full jars, make sure the two jar openings are exactly aligned. Then, holding the top jar, slowly slide the cardboard completely free from the jars. Some water might spill out, but the majority will be trapped between the jars.

You'll notice some slight mixing, but most of the warm water will remain in the top jar. This is because it's less dense, and as in the Sugar Rainbow project (page 85), the less dense liquid will "float" on top of the denser one. This effect will last for several minutes, until the warm water cools. For added fun, see what happens if you redo the experiment with the denser cold water on top.

Fountain of Youth

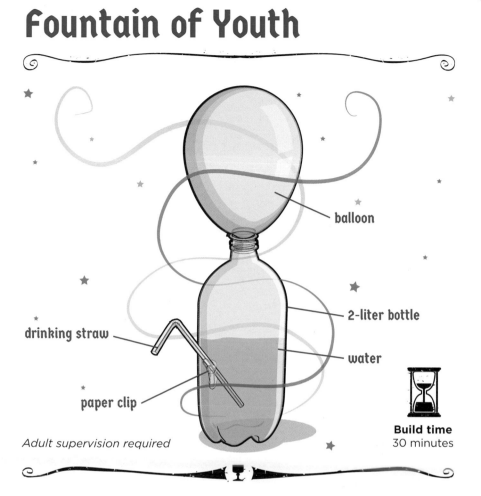

balloon

2-liter bottle

drinking straw

water

paper clip

Adult supervision required

Build time
30 minutes

New students at the School of Labcraft Wizards learn pretty quickly that spellcasting isn't as easy as just waving a wand. Stay alert during tricky magic lessons by keeping this tabletop Fountain of Youth handy! Straight out of a fairy tale, it magically produces water that can restore any weary pupil's youthful vitality!

Supplies
1 medium or large paper clip
1 plastic 2-liter soft drink
   bottle
2 drinking straws with flexible
   heads
Clear tape
Water
1 large balloon

Tools
Needle-nose pliers
Hobby knife
Safety glasses
Ruler
Hot glue gun
Bowl or other container

Step 1

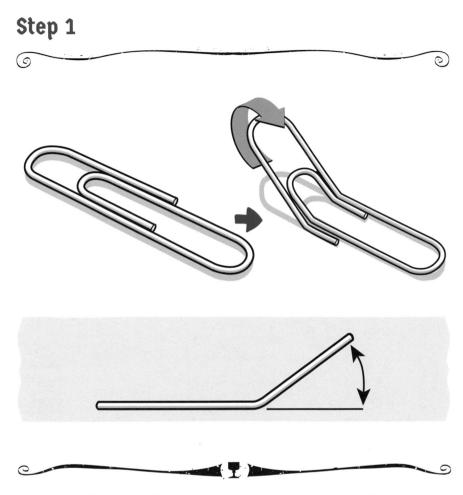

Using needle-nose pliers or a similar tool, bend a medium or large paper clip at the center to a 45-degree angle, as shown.

Step 2

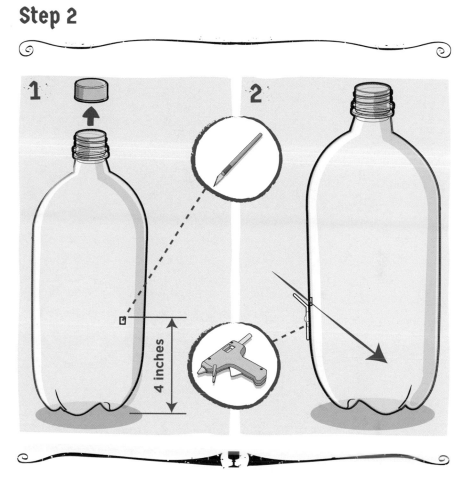

Remove the cap from, rinse, and remove the label from an empty plastic 2-liter soft drink bottle. With a hobby knife, and while wearing safety glasses, carefully cut a small square in the side of the bottle, 4 inches from the bottom, as shown in illustration 1. The square should be the same size as the drinking straw you've chosen, about ³⁄₁₆ inch on each side.

With hot glue, attach the bent paper clip from step 1 to the bottle, so the flat portion is just below the opening and the bent segment slants away from it. When properly positioned, the 45-degree angle of the clip should point toward the bottom of the bottle as shown by the arrow in illustration 2.

Fountain of Youth

Step 3

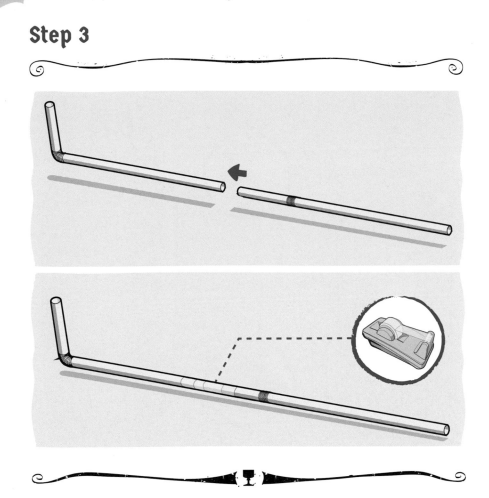

Obtain two drinking straws with flexible heads, and join them together to make one long straw. To do this, squeeze the top of one straw so that it slides into bottom of the other, opposite the bendable head.

Add clear tape around the connection to make the long straw watertight.

Step 4

Slide the straight end of the double-length straw into the small opening in the side of the bottle, resting the straw on the angled paper clip segment. Use hot glue to secure the straw in place and fill in any gaps around it for a watertight connection.

Once the hot glue has cooled, fill the bottle with water. The waterline should not be any higher than the highest point on the end of the bendable straw head, as illustrated on the right.

Step 5

Before bringing the Fountain of Youth to life, place a bowl or other container under the straw head. Make sure it's large enough to hold any water that flows out. To activate, blow up a large balloon, but instead of tying it off, carefully stretch the mouthpiece over the top of the bottle. Once it's attached, the trapped air in the balloon will try to escape. As the air begins to push into the bottle, the water will be pushed out through the attached straw until the balloon completely deflates or the bottle is emptied.

For more fun, use additional straws to extend and alter the water's flow.

Magic Bean

water — jar

bean — paper towel

Build time
2 weeks

Do not let the plain exterior of the Magic Bean fool you! When planted, these pint-sized beans can quickly grow into gigantic beanstalks. For this reason, Magic Beans are also called Wizard Ladders, and spellcasters often carry them around in pouches to aid in climbing unexpected obstacles. Though it takes years to learn how to enchant beans capable of climbing instantly into the clouds, you'll be amazed how quickly you can grow a miniature beanstalk of your own.

Supplies

Small glass jar (or similar see-through container)

Paper towel or napkin

Water

Magic Bean Label (page 231)

Clear tape

Dry beans (pinto beans, red beans, or similar)

Gardening pots with soil (optional)

Wooden dowel or stick (optional)

Twist ties or string (optional)

Magic Bean

187

Step 1

Begin this botany adventure by locating a small glass jar, clear cup, or similar see-through container. The chosen container should be less than 6 inches tall.

Dampen a paper towel or napkin, loosely scrunch it up, and stuff it into the jar, pressing it against the bottom and sides of the glass.

Students are encouraged to tape a Magic Bean Label, found on page 231, to the side of jar.

Step 2

Slide a few dry beans (pinto beans, red beans, or similar from the grocery store) into the jar between the glass and the paper towel, so the crumpled towel holds them in place against the sides of the jar. The more beans you use, the better the chance to see some growth. When positioning the beans, try to space them approximately 1 inch from one another. Add a small amount of water to the jar, lightly moistening both the paper towel and the beans wedged beside it.

The glass garden is ready. Find a warm, sunny spot for the Magic Beans to grow, such as a windowsill.

Step 3

For the next few days, continue adding a small amount of water to keep the beans and towel moist. Eventually you'll see roots grow from the beans, followed by stems. Keep adding water to the jar as the beanstalks grow taller.

To watch the beans mature, transfer them to pots filled with potting soil. For additional beanstalk support, add a wooden dowel or stick to the pot and use twist ties or small pieces of string to fasten the stalk to the dowel.

Wizard Tricks

Moving Star

plate

toothpick

water

Build time
10 minutes

The Moving Star or Toothpick Star is a nifty little wizard trick that commands water to move wood into a recognizable shape. With the wave of a straw, a spellcaster magically transforms five broken toothpicks into a five-pointed star! Perform this spell correctly and you'll be the star of the class.

Supplies
5 wooden toothpicks
Water

Tools
Plate
Drinking straw or eyedropper

Step 1

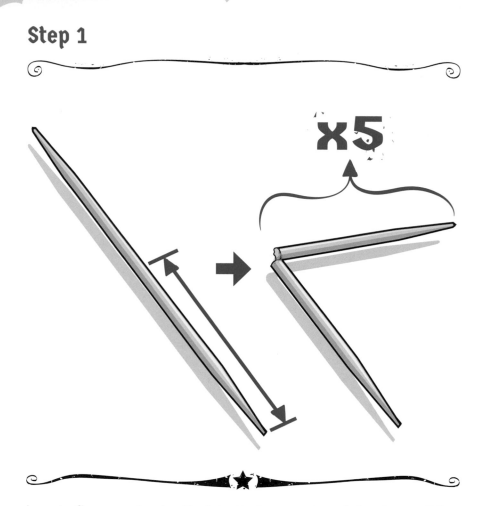

x5

Locate five wooden toothpicks that are new and dry. Snap all five toothpicks exactly in half, into a V shape, but *do not completely separate the two halves*—leave them connected.

Step 2

Find a smooth, flat surface, like a plate. You can use the underside of the plate if the top is curved. Position the five toothpicks symmetrically on the surface so that the broken V edges almost touch in the center, as shown on the left.

Use a straw or eyedropper to pick up a little bit of water, then carefully place a few drops in the middle of the positioned toothpicks. The dry wood will absorb the water molecules, which will travel through the wood fibers via the process called *capillary action*. (It's the same way liquid is pulled up into the cardboard base of the Wizard's Tree on page 132.) This action pulls the water to the ends of all the broken toothpicks.

Step 3

As the water is absorbed, you may need to add a few more drops, but be careful not to submerge the toothpicks. It can take seconds or several minutes, but when the toothpicks have fully absorbed enough water, they will begins to bend and move. As the bends in the wood straighten out, the toothpicks will shift into the shape of a five-pointed star.

Pepper Command

dish soap

water

pepper

Build time
5 minutes

So that they can't be rendered helpless by spells that disarm or silence them, the School of Labcraft Wizards teaches student how to command magic without the use of wands and incantations. To develop this skill, novice wizards must first learn how to channel mystical energies through their fingertips, with a simple wizard trick known as Pepper Command.

Supplies
2 cups of water
1 tablespoon of ground pepper
1 drop of dish soap

Tools
Bowl

Step 1

2 cups

1 tablespoon

The Pepper Command, or Order of the Pepper, is one of the easiest wizard tricks to pull off! It all starts with a bowl filled with approximately 2 cups of water.

Evenly sprinkle 1 tablespoon of ground pepper onto the water's surface.

Step 2

Dip a clean finger into the center of the bowl. Notice that the pepper does not react.

Now, dab a small amount of dish soap onto your fingertip, and dip that finger into the center of the bowl again. Watch the pepper scurry away from your soapy finger.

Why does the pepper move? It's not actually repelled by the soap; instead, it's drawn away because the soap breaks the *surface tension* of the water. Ordinarily, water molecules bond together to create something like a skin on the surface of the water. This skin bulges up a bit in the center of the container. But when soap is added, it ruptures this surface tension, pushing the water and pepper toward the sides of the container.

Step 3

The Pepper Command can also be performed with a magic wand. Place a small amount of liquid dishwashing soap on the tip of your wand, then dip the wand tip into the center of the bowl.

Balloon Skewer

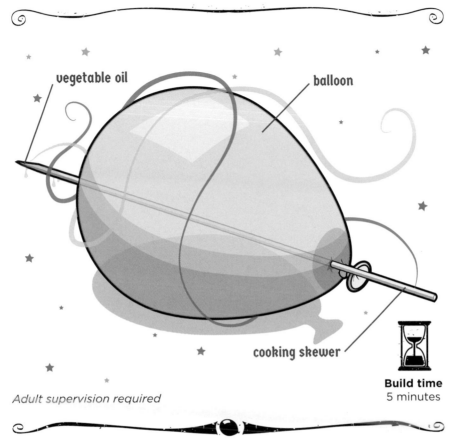

vegetable oil

balloon

cooking skewer

Build time
5 minutes

Adult supervision required

Students must remember that anything can be altered through the power of wizardry, even the relationship between an inflated balloon and large wooden needle. With a quick protective spell, the impossible is suddenly magically possible: piercing the inflated balloon with the wooden needle without the expected *bang!* The Balloon Skewer trick is a perfect group activity, and whether it's cast properly or improperly, it will still be the life of the party!

Supplies
1 latex balloon
1 wooden cooking skewer
   (~10 inches long)
Vegetable oil

Tools
Bowl
Safety glasses

Step 1

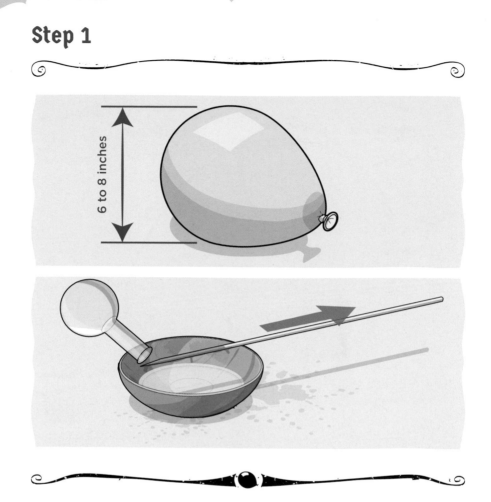

The first step for this amazing enchantment is inflating one latex balloon and knotting it. We suggest inflating the balloon to roughly 6 to 8 inches in diameter—smaller in diameter than the length of your chosen wooden cooking skewer.

Pour a small amount of vegetable oil into a bowl, and use your fingers to coat the pointed end of the wooden skewer with oil. Coat the first few inches of the wooden shaft as well.

Step 2

Don't poke the balloon yet; it's critical to choose the proper points for the wooden skewer to enter and exit the balloon. The entry point should be the area of thick rubber located around the tied-off end of the balloon. While wearing safety glasses, gently press the lubricated point of the skewer through the thick rubber, as shown in the top illustration. A gentle press accompanied by a slow twisting motion may help puncturing the latex.

Next, push the skewer further into the balloon. Guide it toward the ideal exit point: the small dot on the top of the balloon, where like at the entry point the rubber is especially thick. Gently push the skewer through this dot, as shown in the bottom image.

Step 3

The secret to this protective charm is the entry and exit points you've chosen. When a balloon is inflated, the latex stretches to hold the air, but the top and bottom points are the least stretched. When the skewer pierces these areas, the thick rubber helps keep the balloon intact. The oil on the skewer helps it slide more easily, reducing the potential for tears when piercing the balloon.

Was the balloon blown to smithereens? Experiment with different-sized balloons, and try inflating them more or less. Also, try increasing the amount of oil on the wooden skewer. This wizard trick may take a few tries to master, which is part of the fun.

Ping-Pong Levitation

Ping-Pong ball

plastic bottle

drinking straw

Adult supervision required

Build time
20 minutes

In the wizard world, not every shelf or door is designed to be accessed from ground level, so learning how to levitate is an absolute must. Believe it or not, it all starts with a Ping-Pong ball. Ping-Pong Levitation requires only a few simple household materials, and when all they come together, the power to defy gravity will be within your grasp!

Supplies
1 plastic 1-liter bottle with cap
Clear tape
1 drinking straw with flexible
    head
1 Ping-Pong ball

Tools
Scissors
Wooden block (optional)
Safety glasses
Hammer
Large nail
Phillips head screwdriver
Hobby knife (optional)

Step 1

Find a clean plastic 1-liter bottle with a screw-on cap. (A similar-sized bottle can be substituted.) Wrap a piece of clear tape below the bottle's neck, approximately 3½ inches from the mouth of the bottle, or where the expanding neck meets the cylinder, as shown on the left. The tape should be level with the top of the bottle.

    With scissors, use the tape as a cutting guide to remove the top of the bottle. Trim off any sharp edges. The Ping-Pong Levitation trick will use the bottle top; recycle the bottom or save it for growing a Magic Bean (page 187).

Step 2

Place the plastic bottle cap on a work surface you don't have to worry about scratching or puncturing, such as a wooden block. While wearing safety glasses, pound a center hole through the bottle cap with a hammer and a large nail. Remove the nail (illustration 1).

Next, push the end of a large Phillips head screwdriver or similar tool through the hole to increase its diameter (illustration 2). You can also use a hobby knife to increase the diameter and remove any excess material, but **only with the safety glasses and an adult's help**.

Slide the flexible head of the straw into the hole in the bottle cap, until half of it protrudes from the other side (illustration 3). A snug fit is ideal, but if the bottle cap hole is too small, use a hobby knife to increase the diameter. If the hole is too large, add tape around the straw head to wedge it in place.

Step 3

Screw the bottle cap and straw back onto the modified bottle top. Put your lips to the long end of the straw and begin to blow as you place the Ping-Pong ball above the short end of the straw. The flow of air underneath the ball will push it upward until it balances with the force of gravity pulling it down, while the flow of air *around* the ball will keep it centered above the cone-shaped bottle top. The spellcaster's lung capacity will determine how long the ball levitates.

Walking Water

water

food coloring

string

plastic cup

tape

Build time
10 minutes

For all of the wizard world's astonishing achievements, the most remarkable may be this improved method of dispensing liquids. Walking Water, also known as Traveling Water, is a spell that allows water or potions to be poured diagonally. Since some potions are best not to be spilled, a wizard trick that prevents spilling is ingenious—and its antigravity properties will puzzle your non-magical friends.

Supplies

2 disposable plastic cups
Water
24 inches of craft string or
    yarn
Electrical tape or duct tape
Food coloring (a few drops)

Tools

Fork

Step 1

cup 1

cup 2

TAPE

This trick is best performed outside or somewhere else where it's OK to make a mess. Begin by filling a disposable plastic cup with water. Then take a 24-inch length of craft string or yarn and dampen it by soaking it in the filled cup of water.

Tape one end of the presoaked string to the bottom center of a second disposable plastic cup. You will have the best luck using electrical tape or duct tape, but similar tapes or adhesives will work, too.

Step 2

hold

cup 1

Add a few drops of food coloring to the water-filled cup and use a fork to mix them in. Elevate the full cup of water above the second cup. Hold the loose end of the string so that it rests inside the lip of the elevated cup. Move the elevated string and full cup away from the empty cup until the string is tight.

With the ends of the string in each cup, slowly tip the elevated cup to start the water pouring, aiming the water onto the string. The first few drops might not follow the string's diagonal direction, but eventually the water-soaked string will "grab" the poured water, creating a "sticky" path down the string and into the empty cup. That's because molecules of water stick to one another, which is called *cohesion*, and to other surfaces such as the string, which is called *adhesion*. Water sticks better to itself than to other surfaces, which is why you may get a small puddle before enough water has built up on the string.

Step 3

Push the limits of this wizard trick! Experiment with increased string lengths: will the water molecules still stick to the string across the increased travel distance? See if a classmate will feel confident enough to lie underneath the string during your extreme Walking Water attempts.

Spirit Prison

- 2-liter bottle
- balloon
- trash bag
- cereal box
- water
- metal nut
- paper clip

Adult supervision required

Build time
30 minutes

As you reach the end of your Labcraft lessons, you've become a tempting target for dark spirits that feed on magical energies. Fortunately, our final wizard trick, known to non-magical folk as a Cartesian Diver, will teach you how to imprison these bothersome spirits, and even make them float and fall at your command!

Supplies

1 small black latex balloon
1 plastic 2-liter soft drink
   bottle with cap
1 metal nut (~5/16-inch diameter)
1 small paper clip
1 black plastic trash bag
1 sheet of corrugated
   cardboard
Water
1 to 3 small metal washers

Food coloring (optional)
1 empty cereal box

Tools

Safety glasses
Scissors
Wire cutters (optional)
Ruler
Hobby knife
Hot glue gun
Drinking glass

Step 1

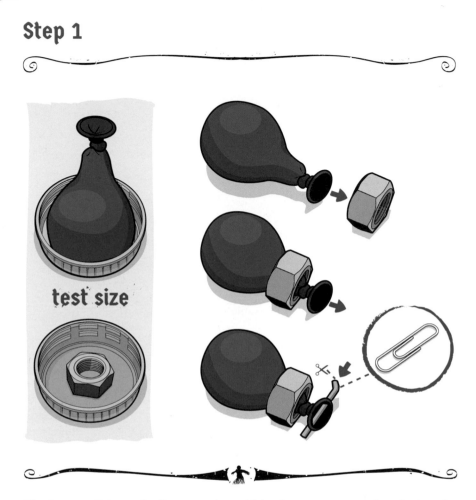

test size

Find a small latex balloon, colored black, to serve as the dark spirit's head. Inflate the balloon, but prior to tying it closed, use the cap of a 2-liter bottle to determine the proper size: the inflated balloon must fit inside the cap, as shown on the left. Balloons larger than the cap will be difficult to insert into the bottle.

Tie off the balloon and add weight to it by sliding a metal nut about 5/16 inch in diameter over the tied collar of the balloon as shown. To fasten the metal nut onto the balloon, put on safety glasses and trim 5/8 inch off a small paper clip using scissors or wire cutters. Pierce the balloon collar as shown, positioning the shortened paper clip at the halfway point in the collar. Hold the balloon upright to confirm that the nut will not fall off.

Step 2

The spirit's long, shadowy body will be constructed out of a black plastic trash bag. Flatten the trash bag out on a sheet of corrugated cardboard or similar safe cutting surface. With a hobby knife, the safety glasses, **and an adult's help**, carefully cut a 7-by-4-inch rectangle. A hobby knife is recommended because cutting a trash bag with scissors can be difficult.

Attach the metal nut onto the top center of the rectangle as illustrated, using a hot glue gun on *low heat*. Do not let the hot glue damage the inflated balloon.

Step 3

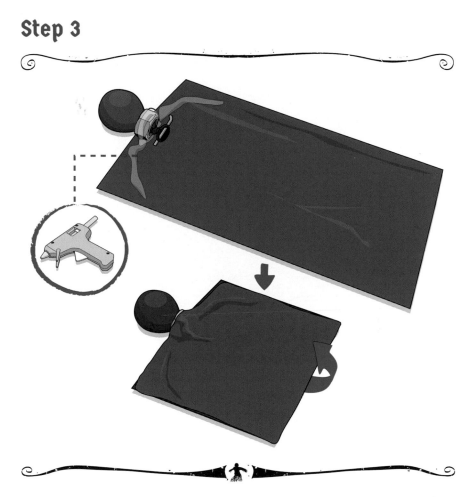

Form the shoulders and upper arms of the dark spirit by adding two lines of hot glue to the trash bag, one on each side of the attached metal nut, as shown in the top illustration. With the glue still hot, fold the plastic rectangle in half, edge to edge, as illustrated on the bottom. Allow the glue to dry.

Step 4

To give the spirit ghostly tendrils for its arms and legs, you'll again use the hobby knife on the corrugated cardboard sheet or other safe cutting surface. First, where the balloon head meets the plastic square, cut the top two corners of the plastic square (illustration 1). The cuts should be wavy and angle downward, and create a hint of shoulder blades.

Next, create the shape of the spirit's body by removing black plastic under the arms on both the right and left side of the captured spirit (illustration 2). Then, use the blade of the knife to cut several lines at the ends of both arms and the bottom of the cloak for a ghostly tendril effect (illustration 3).

Step 5

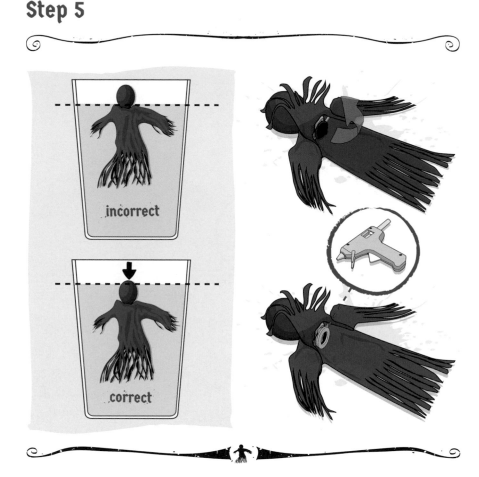

incorrect

correct

Prior to containment, the spirit should be tested for proper *buoyancy*—how well it floats in water. To do this, fill a drinking glass with water and place the spirit inside. Ideally, its head should just barely poke out above the water, as shown in the bottom left illustration.

If the buoyancy is incorrect (top left illustration), you'll need to add more weight. Lift up the front half of the spirit's body to reveal the attached metal nut. Dry the nut and use hot glue to attach a small metal washer to the metal nut. Once the glue dries, test the buoyancy again. Continue adding washers and retesting until the buoyancy is correct.

Step 6

Time to imprison the spirit! Fill the plastic 2-liter soft drink bottle a little more than three-quarters of the way to the top, then slide the spirit into the bottle. Add a few drops of food coloring to resemble an ominous sky, then screw the cap back on, making the bottle airtight.

Cut an empty cereal box with scissors to create a castle wall to wrap around the bottom of the soft drink bottle. Carefully cut out the distinctive castle wall pattern and attach the cardboard to the bottle with hot glue.

Step 7

Watch it fly! With two hands, squeeze the bottle, increasing the pressure inside and causing the dark spirit to drop into the castle in search of magical energies. When you let go, the pressure is released, sending the spirit soaring back into the sky.

7

FROG RIBBITS
MAGIC WANDS

DRAGON EGG
USE WITH CAUTION

Magical Labels

MAGICAL MENDING
OGRE AID SNOT

100% WINGED
JAR OF FAIRIES
FOR HEAVY-
MINDED SLEEPERS

Bottled
BABY KRAKEN
SLIME
LABCRAFT POTIONS

80
STORM
IN A JAR
HANDLE
WITH CARE

GARDEN'S FINEST
SLUGS
USE AS NEEDED

PURE
CRYSTAL
COURAGE
LABCRAFT
POTIONS

WIZARD'S LADDER
MAGIC BEAN
WARNING: GROWS EAST
LABCRAFT POTIONS

Wand Box Labels

For Wand Box project, page 15.
Use a copy machine or scanner to make multiple copies.

Dragon Egg Labels

— For Dragon Eggs project, page 55.

Use a copy machine or scanner to make multiple copies.

Ogre Snot Labels

For Ogre Snot project, page 63.

Use a copy machine or scanner to make multiple copies.

Jar of Fairies Labels

For Jar of Fairies project, page 67.

Use a copy machine or scanner to make multiple copies.

Baby Kraken Slime Labels

For Baby Kraken Slime project, page 71.
Use a copy machine or scanner to make multiple copies.

Storm in a Jar Labels

For Frozen Snowstorm project, page 91. Cloud in a Jar project, page 97, and 2-Liter Tornado project, page 109.

Use a copy machine or scanner to make multiple copies.

Crystal Courage Labels

For Crystal Courage project, page 117.

Use a copy machine or scanner to make multiple copies.

Edible Slugs Labels

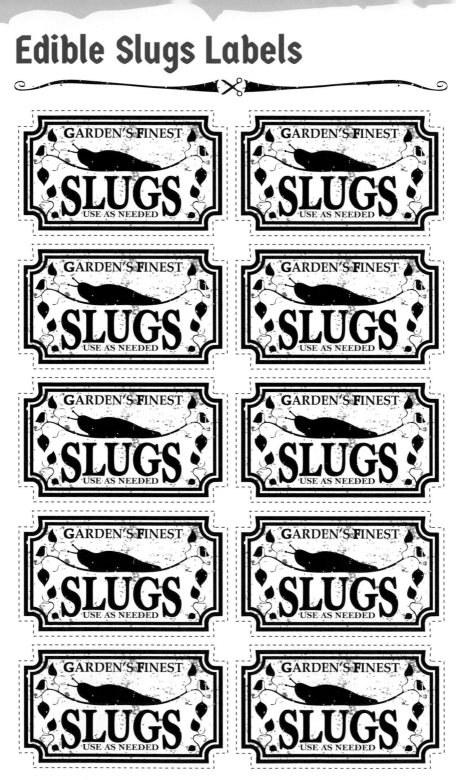

For Brew Slugs project, page 151.
Use a copy machine or scanner to make multiple copies.

Magic Bean Labels

For Magic Bean project, page 187.
Use a copy machine or scanner to make multiple copies.

For more information and free downloadable labels, please visit:

WWW.JOHNAUSTINBOOKS.COM

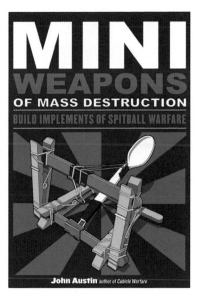

MiniWeapons of Mass Destruction: Build a Secret Agent Arsenal

John Austin

978-1-56976-716-0
$16.95 (CAN $18.95)

If you're a budding spy, what better way to conceal your clandestine activities than to miniaturize your secret agent arsenal? *MiniWeapons of Mass Destruction: Build a Secret Agent Arsenal* provides fully illustrated step-by-step instructions for building 30 different spy weapons and surveillance tools, including:

- Paper Dart Watch
- Rubber Band Derringer
- Pushpin Dart
- Toothpaste Periscope
- Bionic Ear
- Pen Blowgun
- Mint Tin Catapult
- Cotton Swab .38 Special
- Paper Throwing Star
- And more!

Once you've assembled your weaponry, the author provides a number of ideas on how to hide your stash—inside a deck of cards, a false-bottom soda bottle, or a cereal box briefcase—and targets for practicing your spycraft, including a flip-down firing range, a fake security camera, and sharks with laser beams.

MiniWeapons of Mass Destruction: Build Siege Weapons of the Dark Ages

John Austin

978-1-61374-548-9
$16.95 (CAN $18.95)

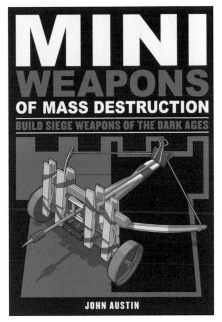

In a world where moats and drawbridges are in short supply, how will you ever defend your turf? Or perhaps you want to expand your realm. *MiniWeapons of Mass Destruction: Build Siege Weapons of the Dark Ages* provides step-by-step instructions on how to turn everyday household and office items into 35 different medieval weapons for the modern era, including:

- ➲ Candy Box Catapult
- ➲ Chopstick Bow
- ➲ Bottle Cap Crossbow
- ➲ Clothespin Ballista
- ➲ Marshmallow Catapult
- ➲ CD Trebuchet
- ➲ Tic Tac Onager
- ➲ Mousetrap Catapult
- ➲ Plastic Ruler Crossbow
- ➲ And more!

Once you've assembled your arsenal, the author provides a number of targets to practice your shooting skills—an empty milk carton is converted into a siege tower, an oatmeal box into a castle turret, and more. Once you're armed and trained, there's no need for your desk, cubicle, or personal space to go undefended. Huzzah!

MiniWeapons of Mass Destruction: Build and Master Ninja Weapons

John Austin

978-1-61374-924-1
$16.95 (CAN $19.95)

To become a ninja master, you need discipline, a silent footstep, and an impressive personal arsenal. Author and toy designer John Austin provides step-by-step instructions on how to turn everyday household and office items into 37 different ninja weapons for the modern era, including:

- ➲ Crouching Tiger Catapult
- ➲ Origami Boomerang
- ➲ Craft Stick Katana
- ➲ Golf Tee Shuriken
- ➲ Cereal Box Blowgun
- ➲ Paper Clip Grappling Hook
- ➲ Magazine Nunchucks
- ➲ Pencil Top Eraser Dart
- ➲ Paper Plate Ninja Star
- ➲ And more!

Once you've assembled an armory, the author provides several targets to practice your shooting skills—nested paper cups become a dragon, chopsticks and a paper plate form a tripod bull's-eye, and more. Armed, trained, and shrouded in black, you are now prepared for missions of reconnaissance and sabotage and other grim errands.

MiniWeapons of Mass Destruction Targets

100+ Tear-Out Targets, Plus 5 New MiniWeapons

John Austin

978-1-61374-013-2
$9.95 (CAN $10.95)

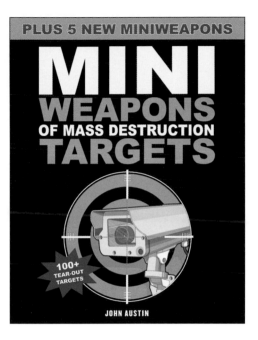

The key to becoming an accomplished marksman is to practice, practice, practice. *MiniWeapons of Mass Destruction Targets* contains more than 100 tear-out targets to develop your skills. The targets are divided into three themes—Basic, Secret Agent, and Dark Ages—with a variety of gameplay scenarios. Blast the lock off a chained door, knock down a castle gate, compete in a game of Around the World, or shoot several miniature targets at various locations. Rules on the back of each target describe basic and advanced play.

In addition to the 100+ targets, MiniWeapons master John Austin provides instructions for building five new MiniWeapons perfect for target shooting:

- ➲ Paper Pick Blow Gun
- ➲ Semiautomatic Pen Pistol
- ➲ Spitball Shooter with Clip
- ➲ Pen Cap Dart
- ➲ Toothpick Tape Dart

Safety instructions are also included, as well as a guide to setting up an in-house firing range that will protect walls and furniture.

So Now You're a Zombie

A Handbook for the Newly Undead

John Austin

978-1-56976-342-1

$14.95 (CAN $16.95)

Zombies know that being undead can be disorienting. Your arms and other appendages tend to rot and fall off. It's difficult to communicate with a vocabulary limited to moans and gurgles. And that smell! (Yes, it's *you*.) But most of all, you must constantly find and ingest human brains. *Braaaains!!!*

What's a reanimated corpse to do?

As the first handbook written specifically for the undead, *So Now You're a Zombie* explains how your new, putrid body works and what you need to survive in this zombiphobic world. Dozens of helpful diagrams outline attack strategies to secure your human prey, such as the Ghoul Reach, the Flanking Zeds, the Bite Hold, and the Aerial Fall. You'll learn how to successfully extract the living from boarded-up farmhouses and broken-down vehicles. Zombiologist John Austin even explores the upside of being a zombie. Gone are the burdens of employment, taxes, social networks, and basic hygiene, allowing you to focus on the simple necessities: the juicy gray matter found in the skulls of the living.

The Art of
the Catapult

Build Greek Ballistae, Roman Onagers, English Trebuchets, and More Ancient Artillery

William Gurstelle

978-1-55652-526-1
$16.95 (CAN $18.95)

"This book is a hoot . . . the modern version of *Fun for Boys* and *Harper's Electricity for Boys*." —*Natural History*

Whether playing at defending their own castle or simply chucking pumpkins over a fence, wannabe marauders and tinkerers will become fast acquainted with Ludgar, the War Wolf, Ill Neighbor, Cabulus, and the Wild Donkey—ancient artillery devices known commonly as catapults. Instructions and diagrams illustrate how to build seven authentic, working model catapults, including an early Greek ballista, a Roman onager, and the apex of catapult technology, the English trebuchet.

Soda-Pop Rockets

20 Sensational Rockets to Make from Plastic Bottles

Paul Jarvis

978-1-55652-960-3
$16.95 (CAN $18.95)

Anyone can recycle a plastic bottle by tossing it into a bin, but it takes a bit of skill to propel it into a bin from 500 feet away. This fun guide features 20 different easy-to-launch rockets that can be built from discarded plastic drink bottles.

After learning how to construct and launch a basic model, you'll find new ways to modify and improve your designs. Clear, step-by-step instructions with full-color illustrations accompany each project, along with photographs of the author firing his creations into the sky.

The Paper Boomerang Book

Build Them, Throw Them, and Get Them to Return Every Time

Mark Latno

978-1-56976-282-0
$12.95 (CAN $13.95)

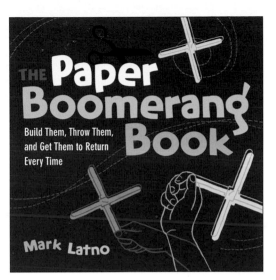

The Paper Boomerang Book is the first-of-its-kind guide to this fascinating toy. Boomerang expert Mark Latno will tell you how to build, perfect, and troubleshoot your own model.

Once you've mastered the basic throw, return, and catch, it's on to more impressive tricks—the Over-the-Shoulder Throw, the Boomerang Juggle, the Under-the-Leg Catch, and the dreaded Double-Handed, Backward, Double-Boomerang Throw. And best of all, you don't have to wait for a clear, sunny day to test your flyers—they can be flown indoors in almost any sized room, rain or shine.

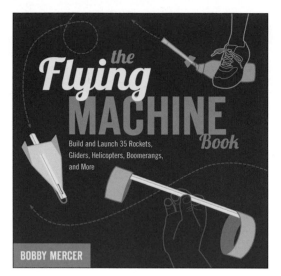

The Flying Machine Book

Build and Launch 35 Rockets, Helicopters, Boomerangs, and More

Bobby Mercer

978-1-61374-086-6
$14.95 (CAN $16.95)

Calling all future Amelia Earharts and Chuck Yeagers—there's more than one way to get off the ground! *The Flying Machine Book* will show you how to construct 35 easy-to-build and fun-to-fly contraptions that can be used indoors or out.

Better still, each of these rockets, gliders, boomerangs, launchers, and helicopters can be made for little or no cost using recycled materials. Rubber bands, paper clips, straws, plastic bottles, and index cards can all be transformed into amazing, gravity-defying flyers, from Bottle Rockets to Grape Bazookas, Plastic Zippers to Maple Key Helicopters. Each project contains a materials list and detailed step-by-step instructions with photos, as well as an explanation of the science behind the flyer. Use this information to modify and improve your designs, or explain to your teacher why throwing a paper airplane is a mini science lesson.

The Hot Air Balloon Book

Build and Launch Kongming Lanterns, Solar Tetroons, and More

Clive Catterall

978-1-61374-096-5

$14.95 (CAN $16.95)

More than a century before the Wright brothers' first flight, humans were taking to the skies in hot air balloons. Today, with basic craft skills, you can build and safely launch your own balloons using inexpensive, readily available materials.

Author and inventor Clive Catterall provides illustrated, step-by-step instructions for eight different homemade models, from the Solar Tetroon to the Kongming Lantern, as well as the science and history behind them. *The Hot Air Balloon Book* also shows readers ways to heat the interior air that lifts these balloons, from tea candles to hair dryers, kitchen toasters to the sun's warming rays.

The Way Toys Work

The Science Behind the Magic 8 Ball, Etch A Sketch, Boomerang, and More

Ed Sobey and Woody Sobey

978-1-55652-745-6
$14.95 (CAN $16.95)

"Perfect for collectors, for anyone daring enough to build homemade versions of these classic toys and even for casual browsers." —*Booklist*

Profiling 50 of the world's most popular playthings—including their history, trivia, and the technology involved—this guide uncovers the hidden science of toys. Discover how an Etch A Sketch writes on its gray screen, why a boomerang returns after it is thrown, and how an RC car responds to a remote control device. This entertaining and informative reference also features do-it-yourself experiments and tips on reverse engineering old toys to observe their interior mechanics, and even provides pointers on how to build your own toys using only recycled materials and a little ingenuity.